# How Should Society Address the Needs of the Elderly?

DATE

MR 30 '06

# Other books in the At Issue series:

# At ✳ Issue

# How Should Society Address the Needs of the Elderly?

Tamara Thompson, *Book Editor*

Bruce Glassman, *Vice President*
Bonnie Szumski, *Publisher*
Helen Cothran, *Managing Editor*

**GREENHAVEN PRESS**
*An imprint of Thomson Gale, a part of The Thomson Corporation*

THOMSON
———✳———
GALE

Detroit • New York • San Francisco • San Diego • New Haven, Conn.
Waterville, Maine • London • Munich

*For more information, contact*
Greenhaven Press
27500 Drake Rd.
Farmington Hills, MI 48331-3535
Or you can visit our Internet site at http://www.gale.com

| LIBRARY OF CONGRESS CATALOGING-IN-PUBLICATION DATA |
| --- |
| How should society address the needs of the elderly? / Tamara Thompson, book editor. |
|     p. cm. — (At issue) |
| Includes bibliographical references and index. |
| ISBN 0-7377-2721-7 (lib. : alk. paper) — ISBN 0-7377-2722-5 (pbk. : alk. paper) |
|    1. Older people—Services for—United States. 2. Older people—Government policy—United States. I. Thompson, Tamara. II. At issue (San Diego, Calif.) |
| HV1461.H693  2005 |
| 362.6'0973—dc22                                    2004059760 |

Printed in the United States of America

# Contents

# Introduction

People live longer today than at any time in history, thanks mostly to improved living conditions and modern medical care. In 1900, life expectancy in the United States was just forty-seven years; today it is more than seventy-seven. As a result, the elderly are the fastest-growing age group in the country. According to the U.S. Census Bureau, over the next three decades, the number of Americans age sixty-five and older will double to nearly 70 million—more than twice the population of Canada.

Another reason that the elderly population will continue to experience such explosive growth is that the baby boom generation, the 76 million people born between 1946 and 1964, is aging. The boomers comprise the nation's largest demographic group, and the first members of this massive cohort have already entered their fifties; the youngest will turn fifty-five in 2019. By 2030, roughly 20 percent of the population will be over sixty-five, compared to less than 13 percent in 2005. Additionally, the number of the oldest old—those over eighty-five— is expected to reach 19 million by 2050. With so many people expected to survive into advanced old age, the demand for long-term-care services is guaranteed. What is less certain is what services will be available and who will—or should—pay for them.

While nearly everyone agrees that elderly people need a wide array of services and supports, there are many differing views about society's responsibility to provide them. Two of the biggest and most contentious programs for the elderly are Social Security, the government's retirement benefit program, and Medicare, the government's health insurance program.

Created by President Franklin Delano Roosevelt as part of the New Deal in 1935, Social Security is the public pension plan administered by the federal government. With 34 million participants, it is the country's largest social program. More than two-thirds of Americans rely on Social Security as their main source of retirement income, and nearly 20 percent count on Social Security as their *only* source of income. Medicare, created in 1965, is the government-run health insurance program for those over sixty-five, and younger, disabled individuals. It pays part of the cost when recipients need medical services or are hospitalized.

Both programs were established by the government as part of a "public safety net" to ensure the health and well-being of elderly people, and both reportedly now face a severe financial crisis. By some accounts, Social Security will be unable to pay benefits beginning in 2014 unless changes are made. Various groups forecast that Medicare will go bankrupt by 2029 or even as early as 2019. Other analysts maintain that Medicare and Social Security do not face serious deficits at all. Most experts do agree, however, that retiring boomers will put a significant strain on both programs because, as the population ages, the number of people who collect benefits from the programs will rise while the number who contribute money will decline sharply.

Deciding how to fix these programs—or whether they need to be fixed at all—is the source of much disagreement between those who favor the public safety net and those who favor free-market solutions based on competition and consumer demand. Those who want to preserve the traditional government "entitlements" of the safety net believe it is the duty of a civilized society to provide for its citizens in their old age, through public benefit programs that provide health care, cash payments, and other support. Those who advocate free-market solutions, on the other hand, believe that individuals should be responsible for their own health and financial needs during retirement or that families should take care of their own members, without help from the government.

The dominant trend at the beginning of the twenty-first century is toward privatization—the transfer of responsibility for traditionally public (government-funded) social and health services to for-profit agencies in the private sector. As social welfare policy analyst Neil Gilbert notes, two powerful forces are meeting to shape this century for American seniors—and younger generations as well. The aging of the baby boom generation is dovetailing with the trend toward privatization and away from the publicly funded social safety net. As Gilbert writes in his book *Transformation of the Welfare State:* "The contracting out of services from the public to the private sector is part of a larger trend in the devolution of responsibility for social welfare from central to local units of government and from local government to community-based private agencies." Indeed, President George W. Bush is pursuing a plan to privatize Social Security, and recent changes to Medicare lead many analysts to believe that program will also be privatized.

The road to privatization is not smooth, however. Many people oppose privatization because they doubt that private companies can be trusted to provide good service when they are trying to make a profit. These people argue that the government is better suited to take care of the elderly because it is not trying to make money and it can be held more accountable for its actions. The basic philosophical difference between those who favor privatization and those who favor government programs underlies most of the recent policy debates concerning services for the aging.

The country faces a crucial choice when it comes to providing for the elderly. It must decide whether the traditional public safety net should remain intact or whether it should be transformed, one program at a time, through privatization. Gerontologist Ken Dychtwald frames the challenge that lies ahead as a question: "Can we muster the resources, intelligence, and determination to plot the best course for our collective future?" The decisions ultimately made will have far-reaching implications for both today's seniors and generations to come. The authors in *At Issue: How Should Society Address the Needs of the Elderly?* represent a wide range of viewpoints in the debate over what services elderly people need and who should pay for them.

# 1

# Society Must Prepare for a Wave of Aging Baby Boomers

## Ken Dychtwald

*Ken Dychtwald is a psychologist and gerontologist. He is the author of ten books on issues of aging, including* Age Wave, *which focuses on the aging of the baby boom generation.*

The aging of the baby boom generation—the 76 million people born between 1946 and 1964—will have major consequences at all levels of society. Because people today live much longer than they used to, this "age wave" will overwhelm society if it does not begin making substantial changes now. The country must prepare to care for a staggering number of elderly who have chronic health problems or dementia, or who are dying. The government must reexamine its health care and social services policies so it can better meet the needs of this unprecedentedly large group of seniors. Society must rethink its ideas about retirement, ageism, and quality of life.

Two powerful forces are building that will transform every aspect of life as we know it. The first, the mass aging of our society (and others throughout the world) may very well be the most extraordinary evolutionary event of all time. Throughout 99 percent of all time humans have walked this planet, average life expectancy was under 18 years. We have never before had a mass population of older people. Until very recently, most people did not age; instead, they died relatively young.

During this past century something tsunamic has begun. As a result of dramatic advances in sanitation, public health, food science, pharmacology, surgery, medicine and, lately, wellness-oriented lifestyle management, most of us will age. We are witnessing the birth of a 21st century "gerontocracy."

## The Coming of the "Age Wave"

When this gero-revolution is joined by the second major force that will dominate the decades to come, the 76 million baby boomers barreling toward maturity, an "age wave" emerges that will soon have the strength and power to create vibrant new social forms and functions and an equally compelling potential for social, financial, political and personal catastrophe. Maturity is about to undergo a revolution like nothing the world has ever seen.

*We are witnessing the birth of a 21st century 'gerontocracy.'*

As we envision these two forces colliding, it would be comforting to be able to assume that our society is prepared and that everything will be fine down the road. We could then believe that all of the social and political issues worthy of debate and discussion have already been at least engaged if not resolved and that the future is in good shape: We have got the right healthcare system, the right political priorities, the right Social Security program, the right roles for retirees, the right approach to intergenerational equity and the right marketplace orientation.

But this is not really the case, and it is increasingly keeping me awake at night; things are not pointed in the right direction at all, and we may be heading for disaster.

When I look toward the future, I can clearly see a variety of train wrecks about to happen—all of which are preventable, but only if we fully understand the relationship between our current decisions and their future outcomes and only if we initiate corrective action now.

What follows is an attempt to characterize the 10 physical,

social, spiritual, economic and political crises we will face as we age in the 21st century.

## A Pandemic of Chronic Disease

We are heading toward a future in which chronic disease, frailty and a variety of long-term health problems will be pervasive. If there is going to be a healthy old age for our generation and our children's, we have got to make several dramatic changes in our approach to healthcare.

First, we must substantially upgrade the amount of support directed toward producing scientific breakthroughs that could eliminate or mitigate the diseases of aging.

Second, we should be ashamed of the fact that although we have 128 medical schools in this country, there is only one department of geriatrics. Standards for basic levels of geriatric competency for the average physician, nurse, pharmacist and physical therapist must be set.

Third, since we now know that many of the conditions of the later years can be prevented, postponed or eliminated through proper lifestyle management and self-care, we must make prevention a core component of our healthcare system.

## Mass Dementia

In this century, we have increased our effectiveness at keeping people alive for decades more than our ancestors ever dreamed of living. We already have 3 million people over the age of 85, and this is the fastest-growing segment of the population. However, we have not done that good a job of seeing to it that these long-lived men and women are functioning with full physical and mental faculties. Today, the dementia rate for the 85+ population is a staggering 47 percent.

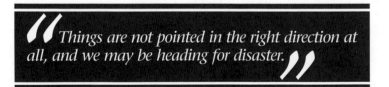

*Things are not pointed in the right direction at all, and we may be heading for disaster.*

We must realize that unless much-needed scientific breakthroughs occur, Alzheimer's will be the scourge of the future—and a costly one at that. For us to inherit a future old age without Alzheimer's, we must take a lesson in political activism from the AIDS and breast cancer crusaders who have dramatically upgraded the amount of attention to and funding for their causes. A revolution in interest, attention and funding for brain dysfunction is needed now. Our future is in the balance.

## The Caregiving Crunch

The average American now has more parents than children (including in-laws and even grandparents), and 10 percent of the elderly population in our country have children who are also elders over 65. We are driving toward a future in which four- and five-generation families will be the norm. As a result, more and more of us will have to provide time, money, respite, housing, transportation, love and nourishment to our parents and our children—and possibly grandchildren and grandparents— simultaneously, for decades.

In response, we need a more effective means of supporting the tens of millions of families who are currently providing care for older family members or friends, a number that is certain to grow. Our health and social services systems will need to include convenient adult daycare, effective homecare and accessible respite care or else millions of caregivers will probably break under the strain. In addition, our work/family benefits and our insurance policies will need to better link and more effectively cover the emerging needs of multiple adult generations.

## Coping with Death and Dying

The contemporary approach to old age and dying emphasizes keeping people alive as long as possible, regardless of their quality of life and regardless of their wishes. Whereas in the past nearly all deaths in America occurred at home, today about 80 percent take place in institutions. Yet, except for a smattering of wonderful hospice programs, we do not have institutions that are sufficiently comforting, nurturing or supportive of the dying and their families. It is essential that we create a palliative-care [hospice] model and make certain it is reimbursed and properly staffed to do an excellent job of respectfully guiding people through this final stage of life.

We will also need a new medical/social/religious ethic within which to allow individuals to feel that their final days are progressing in a fashion that respects their dignity and right to self-determination. Since all recent public polls indicate that the general public and medical professionals are becoming increasingly comfortable with living wills, suicide and passive euthanasia (although assisted suicide and active euthanasia are not viewed positively, for many good reasons), we need enhanced public discussion of these topics to set acceptable policies.

## "Gerassic Park"

All future-oriented public policy in America, including policy regarding Social Security and Medicare, is based on the assumption that there will be no meaningful breakthroughs that will affect longevity or biological aging. So what happens if we wake up tomorrow morning and there is a breakthrough?

Might it be a "Gerassic Park" in which, instead of cloning entire humans, we find a way to clone organs? What if we learn to manipulate the body's immune system to increase longevity? Can we imagine a future without cancer, a world without Alzheimer's or heart disease? It is possible. As biotechnological breakthroughs occur that could radically alter late-life disease and even human aging as we now know it, battles could erupt over who will decide how these mind-boggling technologies will be controlled and who will have access to them.

And if, all of a sudden, people start living to the age of 100 or 120, should they retire and start receiving pensions at 65? What becomes of traditional life-stage activities—work, retirement and old age entitlements? We need public discussion and debate now about the ethical and social repercussions of possible biological and gerontological breakthroughs. The biotechnology century is coming; we should expect the unexpected.

## An Inhospitable Marketplace

Within the U.S. marketplace there still persists an overwhelming obsession with youth. From the perspective of a 60-, 70- or 80-year-old, the world is a long way from being aging-friendly. The typeface in our newspapers and magazines is too small, signage in public buildings and on street corners is too hard to read, doorknobs are too difficult to grasp and turn, traffic lights change too quickly, auditory levels of telephones and televisions are not geared to older ears, lighting in offices creates too much glare, food is not formulated or prepared with older tastebuds in mind, car seats are uncomfortable for older backs, bathtubs are too slippery and dangerous, medications are likely to create pharmacological problems for elders, store personnel are often rude and insensitive to older shoppers, and this list could go on.

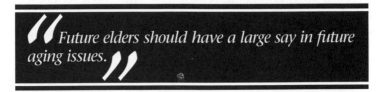

*Future elders should have a large say in future aging issues.*

Most product developers, marketers and advertisers still give only lip service to the needs of the aging population despite the fact that, during the past decade, mature men and women have become the most affluent and active consumers in the history of the American marketplace. We continue to be entranced by the myth that being young is better than being old. If we want a world that fits our needs as we grow older, we must encourage the development of new aging-friendly products in all sectors and match that with much better transgenerational marketing. And, we must take a firm stand to eliminate all ageism in advertising.

## Changing Markers of Old Age

When [German chancellor] Otto von Bismarck picked 65 as the marker of old age in the 1880s, in preparation for Germany's first pension plan, the average life expectancy was only 45. Our current markers of aging have no place in the new millennium. Increasing longevity will not only postpone the arrival of old age, but will also cause all of the stages of life to stretch and shift significantly:

- Youth will become the period from 18–25.
- Young adulthood will expand to include the period from 25–40.
- A new adult life stage, middlescence, will characterize the period from 40–60.
- Late adulthood will be postponed and extended to occupy the period from 60–75.
- Old age will be postponed and extended to begin at 75 and end around 90.
- Very old age will encompass the 90+ life stage.

In addition, the traditional "linear life" paradigm in which people migrate first through education, then work, then leisure/

retirement will become transformed into a new "cyclic life" paradigm in which education, work and leisure are interspersed repeatedly throughout the lifespan. Social and public policy that correspond to life-stage development will have to change to match these more flexible work and retirement styles; at the very least, benefits will need to become more flexible and portable.

## Financial Insecurity

Many of today's elders are the beneficiaries of generous entitlements, radically elevated property values (caused by the boomers) and a responsible savings mentality. In contrast, many boomers have accumulated dangerously high levels of debt and minimal savings and will not be the beneficiaries of a demographically driven home equity boost. Pensions are becoming less reliable as guaranteed benefits are swiftly being replaced by defined-contribution pension plans. The futures of Medicare and Social Security are, at best, shaky. Because of demographic forces, future financial support for boomers in old age is destined to diminish. Eighty percent of boomers do not believe that they will receive a Social Security check. Many boomers are caught in a dangerous state of "financial paralysis." They are not prepared for the future. Therefore, government needs to play an active role in encouraging debate on these issues among all generations, mandating savings and creating flexible, portable pensions. If we do not take action now, we could face a future with massive elder poverty.

## Age Wars

There are profound differences among the old and the young in terms of values, interests, needs and attitudes toward government. Sixty-five-year-olds are reasonably well organized, have a great deal of free time, and have the largest affinity organization in the history of America [the AARP, formerly known as the American Association of Retired Persons], outside of religion, to battle their battles, while 25-year-olds have no political voice and are scrambling to make ends meet.

The boomers will not have much of an impact on modifying today's elders' entitlements. There is too much respect and guilt on the part of boomers and too much power and unity on the part of elders. However, when the boomers amble their way into their 60s, totally disorganized and with financial paralysis, they will become a disproportionately powerful 21st century "gerontocracy" and, with it, will inherit all of the pent-up anger and backlash of the young.

We need to establish a nonpartisan, multigenerational panel so that all age groups have a chance to express the concerns of their stage of life with equal weight and power. Future elders should have a large say in future aging issues.

## Elder Wasteland

We haven't yet figured out the modern purpose of a healthier old age. To what use do we put the incredible resource of elderhood?

We desperately need a heroic model of old age for our coming maturity. If elders want to have the support of younger generations, those generations have also got to feel that elders are giving something back.

We need to establish an elder corps: an army of tens of millions of elder men and women who can become co-teachers in our grade schools, mediators in our churches, mentors in the workplace, surrogate grandparents to our young families, and leaders in our communities. If we had 70-year-olds helping to educate and nourish our children, not only might they be helping them improve their arithmetic skills, but they would also be imparting a powerful base of values that we are about to lose.

Fueled by long sought-after breakthroughs in longevity, we are witnessing the emergence of a gerontocracy, a powerful new old age. And we have the largest generation in American history barreling toward it. How we respond to the demands of this enormous "age wave" and whether or not we are able to avert the catastrophes that might occur in its wake may turn out to be the most important challenge we will face at the dawn of the new millennium.

# 2

# Medicare Reforms Will Benefit Older Americans

## George W. Bush

*George W. Bush is the forty-third president of the United States.*

Medicare is the government health insurance plan that covers all seniors over the age of sixty-five. The Medicare Prescription Drug Improvement and Modernization Act of 2003 was the first substantial change to Medicare since it was created in 1965. The changes were necessary because Medicare had become outdated and no longer helped seniors the way it was intended to. The new law, which will be phased in through 2006, adds prescription drug benefits, gives seniors coverage for preventive health care, and provides a pharmacy discount card. It also allows seniors to establish health savings accounts that will not be taxed. This new law will help today's seniors—as well as those of the future— stay healthy.

*Editor's Note: President Bush delivered the following speech at Spring Valley Hospital in Las Vegas on November 25, 2003, the same day that the U.S. Senate passed the Medicare Prescription Drug Improvement and Modernization Act of 2003. President Bush signed the act on December 8, 2003.*

Today we had a major victory to improve the health care system in America.

The United States Senate has joined the House of Repre-

George W. Bush, remarks at Spring Valley Hospital, Las Vegas, Nevada, November 25, 2003.

sentatives in passing historic reform of Medicare that will strengthen the system, that will modernize the system, that will provide high quality care for the seniors who live in America.

I want to thank and congratulate the members of Congress for their hard work. You see, we have a responsibility in Washington, D.C., to solve problems, not to pass them on. And today, the United States Congress met its responsibility.

We inherited a good Medicare system. It has worked, but it was becoming old and needed help. Because [of] the actions of the Congress, because [of] the actions of members of both political parties, the Medicare system will be modern and it will be strong. . . .

## Best Health Care in the World

This nation's health care is great. We've got the best health care in the world, and we need to keep it that way. We've got a great health care system because of our docs: well-trained, decent, caring people who practice medicine. We've got a great health care system because of our nurses, who work hard to provide compassionate care. We got the best research in the world. We're on the leading edge of change in America.

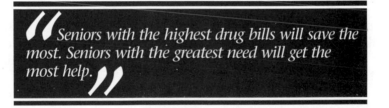

*Seniors with the highest drug bills will save the most. Seniors with the greatest need will get the most help.*

And we got to keep the system vibrant and we must keep it the best in the world, which we intend to do in Washington, D.C. We started out by making sure our seniors have got a modern system. The Medicare system, first of all, is an essential commitment of the federal government. Our federal government has made a commitment to our seniors that we'll provide them an up-to-date, decent health care system. It's a basic trust that has been upheld throughout the generations. And we're keeping that trust by making sure the system works, by making sure that our seniors are well-treated.

[In] recent years, Medicare has not kept up with the advances of modern medicine. In other words, it hasn't met the trust that the federal government has promised to our seniors. Remember, when Medicare was passed in 1965, health care meant house calls and surgery and long hospital stays. And the system was designed to meet the health care delivery systems of the day.

## Changing with the Times

Modern medicine today now includes preventative care, outpatient procedures and at-home care. Many invasive surgeries are now unnecessary because of the new prescription drugs which are being developed.

You know, many Americans have coverage for these new forms of health care and that's positive and we need to keep it that way. Yet seniors who rely exclusively on Medicare do not have the coverage, for many of the new treatments, and do not have coverage for prescription drugs. In other words, medicine changed and Medicare didn't. And as of today, Medicare's changing.

Let me give you an example of the need for modernization. The health care providers here know these examples only too well. Medicare is willing to pay $28,000 for a hospital stay for ulcer surgery. But it won't pay the $500 for the anti-ulcer drugs that would keep the senior out of the hospital in the first place.

Those examples—or that example, like many others, says to me we had a problem with the Medicare system. It doesn't make any sense to pay the $28,000 at the end of the process, but not the $500 up front to keep the $28,000 from happening in the first place.

Medicare should cover medications to keep our seniors out of the hospitals. The new bill does this.

An important part of the reform is to recognize that medicine has changed. It will save our government and the taxpayers money by providing prescription drugs early, so we don't have to pay for it in long hospital stays or invasive surgeries.

## Bill Encourages Competition

Most seniors have got some form of prescription drug coverage from a private plan. And that's important. It's a fact of life here in America. Those plans, however, are becoming less available. We've got to make sure the private sector remains vibrant. The bill I'm about to describe to you does that.

Medicare was very slow to take advantage of new medical advances besides prescription drugs. In other words, you had to go to a bureaucracy in order to get certain procedures covered. Bureaucracies don't move very quickly. They tend not to be very sympathetic organizations. They're not consumer-driven; they're process-driven. They're hidebound by rules and regulations.

*Every American, old and young, will be able to have a health savings account.*

The docs here know what I'm talking about. You get to deal with bureaucracies. It must be frustrating. Sometimes it's a frustrating experience to try to change bureaucracies.

The Medicare plan that I'm going to sign understands that a lack of competition meant that there was no real need to provide innovation. And so we're helping to change the system by giving seniors more options and more choices.

See, members of Congress have got choices. They get to choose from a health care plan. And it works quite well. The three congressmen here would tell you, they're probably pretty satisfied with the plan, if they've chosen to be in it. In other words, you get to choose.

## New Bill Offers Choices

This new Medicare bill I'm going to sign says seniors are plenty capable of making choices themselves. I used to say, "If it's good enough for the members of Congress to have choice, it ought to be good enough for the seniors in America to have choice." Now they're going to have choice, thanks to the bill I'm going to sign.

It's going to take awhile for this piece of legislation to kick in. It'll take about two years [by 2006] to get all the reforms in place.

But within six months of the law being signed, our seniors will start to see real savings in health care costs, because seniors will be eligible for a drug discount card that will save them between 10 to 25 percent off their regular drug costs.

And low-income seniors will receive up to $600 a year to

help them with their drug costs, in addition to the card. Their card will serve as a transition to the reforms that are inherent in the Medicare legislation. When the full drug benefit arrives in 2006, all seniors will be eligible for prescription drug coverage for a monthly premium of about $35. The result is that for most seniors without coverage today the Medicare drug plan will cut their annual drug bills roughly in half. That's positive news for America's seniors. . . .

Seniors with the highest drug bills will save the most. Seniors with the greatest need will get the most help. Low-income seniors will pay a reduced premium or no premium at all and lower or no co-payments for their medications.

Under the new reforms, seniors, as I mentioned, will have choices. You see, some seniors don't want to choose and I can understand that. In other words, people [who] are on Medicare, just don't want to be confronted with a choice.

And the system and the bill we passed recognizes that.

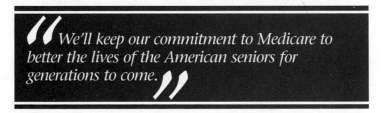

*We'll keep our commitment to Medicare to better the lives of the American seniors for generations to come.*

You can understand why. Person's up in years, and they're just pretty comfortable. They don't want to have to change. Change makes some people nervous and we understand that. And so, should seniors want to stay in traditional Medicare and receive a prescription drug benefit, they will now be able to do so. That's one of the key reforms in the bill.

But other seniors want to choose. They want to be able to make a selection based upon their own particular needs. Some might want protection from high out-of-pocket medical expenses. Some might want expanded coverage for hospital stays. Some might want to be able to pick a plan that better meets their own individual needs.

## Plan Is Demand Driven

And under this law choices will be readily available for our seniors, and that's an important part of reform. Because you see when seniors or any citizen makes a demand, the system responds. If there is a demand-driven system, it means the doctor-patient relationship is going to be more firm and it means people will have better choices to meet their own particular needs.

Some seniors may want the coverage that comes with managed care plans. Medicare Plus Choice [is a managed-care plan]. . . . Under the law, Medicare Plus Choice will be strengthened, not starved. It is a viable option for our seniors around the country. In other words, people will have more control over their health care options, and health care plans will start competing for their business. And that's positive, positive for the consumers, positive for the seniors of America.

## Complete Exams at Sign-Up

There are other important reforms in this bill. When seniors sign up for Medicare, they will get a complete health examination so that doctors can know their health needs from the start. We're finally beginning to focus on preventative care. Makes sense to include preventative care in any health care reforms. The health care providers here know that better than anybody. The bill provides incentives for companies to keep the existing coverage they provide for senior retirees.

There was some concern in Washington—and legitimate concern as far as I'm concerned—that a Medicare reform plan would encourage employers to not do their responsibility to their former retirees. This bill addresses that.

Two out of every three seniors is now covered by some form of private coverage. And the bill addressed the issue, and to make sure that that coverage is still a viable alternative in the marketplace.

Every American, old and young, will be able to have a health savings account. They will be able to put money aside tax-free to help their families with medical expenses. Medical savings accounts are [an] important part of reform. Medical savings accounts trust the consumers, provides incentives for people to make wise choices and helps to maintain the doctor-patient relationship.

This bill helps rural hospitals. . . . Rural hospitals need help to continue to serve our country. This bill sets fair reimbursement rates for doctors serving Medicare patients.

This is a good bill and I'm looking forward to signing it.

Last Saturday's vote in the House and today's vote in the

Senate marks a historic moment, a bipartisan achievement that all Americans can be proud of.

Year after year, the problems in the Medicare system were studied and debated. And yet nothing was done. As a matter of fact, they used to call Medicare "Mediscare" for people in the political process. Some said Medicare reform could never be done. For the sake of our seniors, we've gotten something done. We're acting. We acted on principle in Washington, D.C. We're providing new treatments and new choices. We'll get prescription drug coverage they deserve. We'll keep our commitment to Medicare to better the lives of American seniors for generations to come.

I appreciate the hard work of the members of the Congress. This was a tough bill. People worked hard on it. A lot of people searched their soul on this complex and important piece of legislation. But they stayed after it, stayed focused on the people. A lot of members put politics aside, which we need to do in Washington, D.C., when we're talking about the people's business. I appreciate the seniors and the seniors' groups, such as the AARP [formerly known as the American Association of Retired Persons] who lobbied hard on behalf of a modern Medicare system. People made their opinions known. They let the members know where they stand. And it worked. And it helped. And I'm honored to put my signature on this historic piece of legislation.

# 3

# Medicare Reforms Should Go Much Further

## Jacob S. Hacker and Mark Schlesinger

*Jacob S. Hacker is an assistant professor of political science at Yale University and a fellow at the New America Foundation, a nonpartisan, nonprofit public policy institute. Mark Schlesinger is a professor of public health at Yale and editor of the* Journal of Health Politics, Policy, and Law. *In 2003 he directed a study of private plans in Medicare for the National Academy of Social Insurance.*

More than 35 million seniors receive Medicare, a government health plan that pays part of the cost when they visit a doctor or go to the hospital. The program was created in 1965 and is badly in need of reform. However, recent changes—specifically, the Medicare Modernization and Improvement Act of 2003 (MMIA)—will not solve Medicare's problems and are likely to worsen its financial situation. MMIA undermines Medicare instead of strengthening it because it allows private insurance and drug companies to have too much influence over how the program's benefits are delivered. Medicare does a better job of containing costs and providing services than private companies can. The elderly can best be served by Medicare if the program is opened up to everyone, regardless of age. This would lighten Medicare's burden of covering so many individuals with high-cost medical problems (the elderly) and would distribute costs more evenly among all participants. Such a reform would also eliminate the problem of young workers having to pay for the health care of elderly people. Providing universal health care for all Americans should be the natural evolution of the Medicare program.

A cross the political spectrum, alarm bells are ringing about Medicare, America's giant health program for the aged and disabled. To conservatives, Medicare is a huge, Kremlin-esque bureaucracy destined to soak up more and more of the American economy. To critics on the left, it's an inadequate program that nonetheless siphons off increasingly limited funds that could be used to broaden coverage for children and working families.

The White House–backed Medicare reforms passed late last year [2003] only confirmed each side's worst fears, promising a meager and ill-designed drug benefit at a hugely inflated price. While millions go without basic coverage and budget deficits explode, critics asked how we can countenance pouring hundreds of billions of dollars into a system for the aged that already provides pretty decent protection.

## Building Up Medicare Is the Answer

Here's how: Make improvement and expansion of Medicare the route to universal health coverage in the United States. Medicare does badly need upgrading. Medicare does do too little to help the non-elderly. But the solution isn't to tear down Medicare; it's to build up the program to make it a stable foundation for providing health care for all Americans without access to good workplace coverage. In all the talk about skyrocketing health costs and the uninsured, everyone seems to have forgotten about the one program that can realistically get America to affordable universal insurance in the coming decades.

Ironically, the potential for expanding Medicare to all Americans owes much to past initiatives—mostly pursued by conservatives—that have enhanced beneficiaries' enrollment in private health plans. For all their shortcomings, these proposals have made it possible for Medicare to offer a broad array of private plans, as well as traditional fee-for-service insurance, to young and old alike. But this strategy will succeed only if Medicare also continues to provide the broad risk sharing that is vital to the program's long-standing success—and to the future of American health insurance.

## Medicare Has Faced Heavy Criticism

For a program so loved by the public that even anti-government ideologues tread lightly around it, Medicare has come in for a surprisingly heavy critical barrage. The fusillade consists of two main volleys: that America can't afford Medicare and that the program is built on an irremediably antiquated model. Each of these claims is arresting and superficially attractive. Yet each is wrong, both in its diagnosis and in its prescriptions.

Affordability is the more bipartisan concern—and the one with the stronger basis in fact. The aging of America and the rise of health costs promises to make Medicare much more expensive in the future. According to some estimates, Medicare could represent as much as 7 percent of the economy in 2050, up from about 3 percent today [2004].

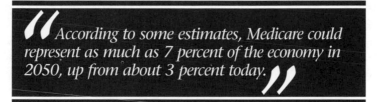

*According to some estimates, Medicare could represent as much as 7 percent of the economy in 2050, up from about 3 percent today.*

All of this is cause for concern, but by no means despair. In the last half-century, the United States has experienced swings in social spending much larger than those predicted by even the direst estimates, with nothing like the crises now prophesied. More important, while Medicare will cost more in the future, Americans will also be much richer, allowing them to devote a larger share of income to it. The issue isn't whether we can pay for Medicare; it's whether we want to. And polls resoundingly indicate that nearly all Americans do.

## Medicare's Financial Crisis Is an Illusion

What's more, the frightening image of Medicare sucking away nearly a tenth of the national income isn't likely to materialize. Every previous Medicare spending "crisis" has prompted serious and effective efforts to rein in costs without cutting benefits. A number of European countries, moreover, are much farther along the demographic road to gerontocracy than is the United States, yet have still sustained their publicly funded health benefits without having medical spending take a larger share of the national income or restricting access for older patients to a level below Medicare's current coverage.

Lurking beneath claims about affordability is the seemingly fixed American belief that all government programs are less efficient and more costly than their private counterparts. That's simply not true of Medicare. In fact, Medicare has contained its spending better than has private insurance over the past two decades. Nor have politicians given away the bank to older Americans. Medicare is remarkably less generous than typical private health plans. A private plan with Medicare's current benefit package would cost about $2,300 for a single non-aged adult, compared with a current average for private plans of about $3,600 with the sort of benefits negotiated at the typical workplace.

Of course, to some, this is the real problem: Medicare is just an outdated model, period. The complaints take many forms—Medicare has an antique payment policy, it doesn't effectively "manage" care, it makes patients pay too much out of pocket—but most of these criticisms boil down to a simple battle cry: Medicare needs radical modernization to encourage competition and incorporate the private sector more fully.

## The Managed-Care Backlash

This call was most alluring during the mid-1990s, when managed-care enthusiasts promised that their plan would decisively rein in costs and stimulate innovative service delivery. Of course, that was before the managed-care backlash sent private insurers scurrying back to arrangements that allow free choice of providers and require cost sharing by patients—in short, the very model that old-fashioned Medicare has retained all along.

*There is nothing inherent in the Medicare model that makes these innovations less possible than in the private sector.*

Medicare could certainly be a more effective insurance program. It should better manage chronic medical conditions, for example, and provide more extensive preventive outreach and better coverage of rehabilitative services. But there is nothing inherent in the Medicare model that makes these innovations less possible than in the private sector. And when it comes to providing timely access to care and financial security, recent surveys of Americans' health-care experiences suggest that conventional Medicare considerably outperforms the average private insurance policy.

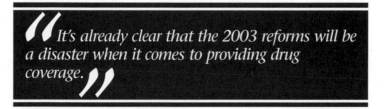

*It's already clear that the 2003 reforms will be a disaster when it comes to providing drug coverage.*

Indeed, it's crucial to recognize that today's Medicare is very different from the model of 30 or 40 years ago. That's because Medicare now allows beneficiaries to choose among a growing variety of private managed-care and fee-for-service options. And these choices meet with overwhelming popular approval: Two-thirds of all Americans favor giving Medicare beneficiaries a choice among insurance plans so long as this does not increase the cost of staying in the conventional Medicare program.

## Private Plans Prove to Be a Mixed Blessing

But wait, haven't private health plans failed Medicare? Stories of them pulling out in droves and increasing deductibles certainly suggest so. But the disruptions of recent years can be exaggerated. At its peak, the turnover rate of plans in Medicare was about the average experienced in the much-lauded Federal Employees Health Benefits Program. Meanwhile, the rewards that private plans have delivered to the program are often neglected. For many beneficiaries who have enrolled in private plans, the broader coverage and coordination of care that private plans can offer has been a boon.

Still, private plans have caused special problems for Medicare's beneficiaries. The aged are an especially difficult group to offer a choice of health plans, not so much because their average costs are higher but because those costs are especially concentrated and catastrophic. This creates a powerful incentive to "cream skim" the healthy and exclude those with more serious and costly health-care needs.

Churning of private plans in and out of Medicare also hits

the elderly and disabled particularly hard because it tends to disrupt the continuity of care that is essential for effective treatment of chronic problems. And most of the elderly now in Medicare have little familiarity with private plans, limiting their ability to anticipate these sorts of problems.

## Payment System Needs to Be Fixed

Fixing Medicare's system for paying private plans would help considerably. Currently, Medicare essentially pays all plans that want to participate in each region the same amount—pegged to the average cost of seniors in the traditional fee-for-service program. The incentives for plans are clear: attract healthier patients, and enter only regions where payments are high. The goal should instead be a level playing field in which plans attract patients only by delivering things that beneficiaries find of value—convenience, coordination, integrated benefits, low cost sharing—not by gaming the system.

A level playing field is decidedly not, however, what the 2003 Medicare legislation contained. It's already clear that the 2003 reforms will be a disaster when it comes to providing drug coverage. But as bad as the drug benefit is, the way in which the bill coddles the private sector is even more troubling. Under the legislation, private plans will get huge new subsidies to encourage their participation in the program, even though recent studies indicate that private plans continue to be overpaid when the healthier mix of patients they enroll is taken into account.

## Medicare Has No Bargaining Power on Drug Costs

If that weren't enough, drug coverage under the bill must be provided by private insurers. Except in regions where private plans don't emerge, beneficiaries cannot get drug coverage through Medicare itself. And even in such regions, Medicare is prevented from actually serving as a purchaser—it bears the risk, but farms out management to the private sector. This also means, of course, that Medicare has no bargaining power under the bill to hold down skyrocketing drug costs.

Fixing Medicare to correct these egregious overpayments and to allow it to provide drug coverage directly is essential. But there's another important step that could and should be taken to make private plans in Medicare work better: Expand it to the non-aged. Doing so would greatly even out the costs among subscribers by bringing in healthier younger Americans. It would reduce the prevalence of chronic illness among enrollees and introduce into Medicare a group of comparatively savvy consumers. Above all, it would make insurance more secure and affordable for all Americans, ensuring that workers and their families have access to a low-cost policy providing free choice of doctors and an effectively regulated system of private health plans.

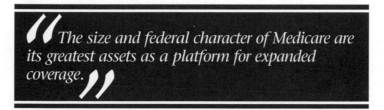

*The size and federal character of Medicare are its greatest assets as a platform for expanded coverage.*

If the goal of expanding Medicare seems radical or strange, remember that when Medicare was enacted in 1965, almost everyone saw it as the first step to universal coverage. That didn't happen, of course, and now advocates of expanded insurance hardly talk about the program—or even see it as an obstacle. Yet, just as in 1965, Medicare remains today the most effective, most attractive, most viable avenue to reach universal health insurance in the United States.

It's also a big and costly federal program, which may be why advocates of universal coverage seem so reluctant to seize on its untapped potential. But this is exactly backward: The size and federal character of Medicare are its greatest assets as a platform for expanded coverage. State insurance programs vary greatly from state to state. Worse, they're "pro-cyclical," meaning they increase their spending when the economy is good and cut it back precisely when the need is greatest. These are not attractive features when trying to ensure health security, and neither would be true of a national program.

## Medicare Remains Highly Popular

The assumption that Americans wouldn't accept a huge federal program called Medicare seems convincing—until one realizes that there already is such a program, it's called Medicare, and Americans absolutely love it. Medicare is among the most consistently popular programs in the United States, and its popularity has been enhanced by the addition of private-plan options, despite the evident problems with their implementation.

Indeed, many Americans don't even think of Medicare as a government program, as is suggested by the story of an elderly constituent who reportedly jumped up at a congressional town-hall meeting and declared, "Keep government out of my Medicare." Which is precisely why the program is such a good institutional route for expanding health coverage. Public-opinion postmortems suggested that Americans turned against Bill Clinton's health plan because Republicans were able to portray it as unfamiliar, unpredictable, and threatening. Medicare would not be vulnerable to the same attack.

But isn't Medicare the sort of dreaded single-payer plan that would place the government in charge of the entire health system? That might have been an effective retort a decade or two ago, but it's hardly relevant to the program that exists today, with its extensive private-plan options. Since polling on health care began during the 1930s, the public has been fairly evenly divided between approaches that rely on public and private insurance. Medicare, in its contemporary form, offers a balance between the two.

## A Prescription for Medicare Reform

Essentially, the reform policy we have in mind would give employers the option of either providing basic coverage on their own or paying a premium based on their total payroll to purchase Medicare coverage for their workers. With the premium set at 5 percent of wages, estimates show that about 40 percent of Americans would be enrolled in Medicare, with the rest in employment-based health plans. The net cost would be roughly $85 billion. This compares favorably to [2004 presidential candidate] John Kerry's plan, which would cover substantially fewer Americans for about $70 billion.

## Opening Medicare to the Young Would Solve Many Problems

Making Medicare available to all Americans would, in a single stroke, address many of the complaints that critics have raised. Though requiring new financing up front, this would greatly *lessen* Medicare's long-term cost problem because it would make program spending less sensitive to the demographic distribution of the American population. By increasing the share of health spending financed by Medicare, it would also give the government greater leverage to control costs. And by bringing in younger Americans, it would make it much easier to improve the program's reliance on private health plans.

But perhaps most crucial, expanding coverage to the uninsured through Medicare would powerfully link the health security of the aged and non-aged. No longer would young workers without insurance shell out payroll taxes to support elderly citizens with good coverage. And no longer would advocates of expanded insurance coverage feel that improving Medicare was at odds with their ultimate aims. Instead of simply making Medicare more like insurance for workers, *this* Medicare reform strategy would also make insurance for workers more like Medicare: secure, affordable, and simple.

To be sure, none of this would be easy. So far has Medicare drifted from the larger goal of universal coverage that advocates rarely mention the two in the same sentence. But the two should be spoken of together, for Medicare's future and the future of American health insurance are necessarily intertwined. The only question is whether Medicare and universal coverage will hang together or hang separately. We can preserve and improve Medicare for future generations and finally make health insurance secure for all Americans. Or we can leave each bobbing separately in a sea of hostility to the ideal of a shared fate that once fired enthusiasm for Medicare—and could do so yet again.

# 4

# Social Security Should Be Privatized

## Daniel Patrick Moynihan and Richard Parsons

*Daniel Patrick Moynihan and Richard Parsons were co-chairs of the President's Commission to Strengthen Social Security. Moynihan, a democratic senator from New York, died in 2003. Parsons is chief operating officer of the AOL/Time Warner media company.*

In May 2001, President George W. Bush created a bipartisan, sixteen-member commission to study the ailing Social Security system and make recommendations about how to modernize it and solve its financial problems. The commission agreed with the president that allowing workers to invest part of their Social Security money in personal retirement accounts is the best way to keep the program healthy so that it can provide retirement benefits for future generations of seniors. Money in the accounts could be invested in the stock market, mutual funds, or bonds. Privatizing Social Security in this way would give individuals more ownership over their futures and allow them to earn higher interest on their retirement money. The Bush administration is considering three privatization models proposed by the commission.

From the first, Social Security was a work in progress. It remains so now. In 1939, just four years after enactment, the Administration and Congress added major provisions. FDR [President Franklin Delano Roosevelt] called for more. As he signed the 1939 Amendments he stated: "We must expect a

Daniel Patrick Moynihan and Richard Parsons, *Strengthening Social Security and Creating Personal Wealth for All Americans*, Report of the President's Commission, December 2001.

great program of social legislation, as such as is represented in the Social Security Act, to be improved and strengthened in the light of additional experience and understanding." He urged an "active study" of future possibilities.

One such possibility—personal retirement accounts that would endow workers with a measure of wealth—has emerged as the central issue in the ongoing national debate over social insurance.

There are a number of reasons for this. The first is the most obvious, if perhaps the least commented upon: Social Security retirement benefits are no longer the bargain they once were. There is nothing sinister about this. Early retirees benefited from the fixed formula of retirement benefits. For years the Social Security Administration would distribute photographs of Ida May Fuller of Ludlow, Vermont, who having paid $24.75 in Social Security taxes lived to age 100 and collected $22,889 in benefits.

In Miss Fuller's time there were almost 42 covered workers for each Social Security beneficiary. We are now down to 3.4 workers per beneficiary. As a result, Social Security as a retirement measure has become a poor investment. It is, even so, an essential *insurance* program. Widows and dependent children are very reliant on dependent benefits. For widows, widowers, singles and children, the monthly check can be a steady, stabilizing factor in life. That said, however, Social Security actuaries estimate that, for a single male worker born in 2000 with average earnings, the real annual return on his currently scheduled contributions to Social Security will be only 0.86 percent. This is not what sends savers to savings banks. For workers who earn the maximum amount taxed (currently $80,400, indexed to wages) the real annual return is *minus* 0.72 percent. This should come as no surprise. Demography is a kind of destiny.

## Learning from the Past

The founders of Social Security always assumed it would be supplemented by individual forms of savings. (In his original Message to Congress, President Roosevelt envisioned pensioners owning annuities.) In the first instance, savings took the form of housing; government subsidies were created in the 1930s, followed by the enormous influence of Veterans Administration mortgages following World War II. By 2000, two-thirds—67.4 percent—of Americans owned their homes.

The [stock market] Crash of '29 left an indelible mark on the generation that lived through it—and for that matter, the one that followed, such that direct investment in markets was slow in returning. But eventually it did. Partly as a consequence of 1929, we have learned a great deal about how a modern economy works. During the Depression, the Federal government did not even calculate the unemployment rate; it was taken every ten years in the Census. Today, our economic statistics are extraordinary in range and accuracy, and since enactment of the Employment Act of 1946 economic policies have, on balance, been successful. The great swings in economic activity have been radically mitigated. In November 2001, the Dating Committee of the National Bureau of Economic Research gave out its judgment that the period of economic expansion that began in March 1991 ended in March 2001. Such a ten-year period of uninterrupted growth is something never before recorded. There will continue to be ups and downs, and all manner of risks, but in the main the modern market economy appears to have settled down to impressive long-term growth.

## The Birth of Mutual Funds

The post–World War II growth period was reflected, naturally enough, in the stock market. More important, a new form of investment, the mutual fund, was developed which enabled small savers to "pool" their investments over a range of stocks and bonds. As reported by the Investment Company Institute, "As of May 2001, 93.3 million individuals, representing 52 percent of all U.S. households owned mutual funds." Further, "Nearly half of mutual fund shareholders have household financial assets below $100,000; 29 percent have less than $50,000."

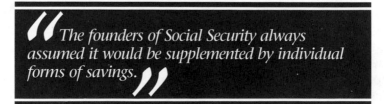

*The founders of Social Security always assumed it would be supplemented by individual forms of savings.*

The surge in the mutual fund ownership began in the early 1980s. One of the more notable innovations was the development of a similar fund, the Thrift Savings Plan, as part of the retirement arrangements for Federal employees. The legislation was enacted quietly by Congress and signed by President Reagan in 1986. In terms of the markets, the timing could not have been better. The results have been stunning, as the Commission learned from testimony by the Director of the Federal Retirement Thrift Investment Board, Roger Mehle. Three funds were available, in whatever combination the employee chose. . . .

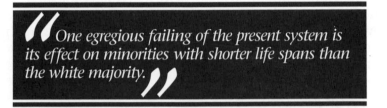

*One egregious failing of the present system is its effect on minorities with shorter life spans than the white majority.*

As of September 2001, 86.6 percent of all Federal employees participated in the program. It is a singular success.

## The Need for Checks and Balances

Martha Derthick's classic study *Policy Making for Social Security* begins with a quotation from Arthur Altmeyer, who was chief executive of the program from 1937 to 1953:

> Social Security will always be a goal, never a finished thing because human aspirations are infinitely expandable . . . just as human nature is infinitely perfectible.

This would not quite have been the view of the Founders, who though human nature to be anything but "infinitely perfectible." Hence checks and balances were needed to make up for the "defect of better motives." And indeed some things, notably demography, proved anything but perfectible. The Social Security tax (F.I.C.A. for Federal Insurance Contribution Act) began at two percent and has been raised more than twenty times, reaching the present 12.4 percent. This is a regressive tax that is paid on the first dollar of income by rich and poor alike. In fact, as of 1997, 79 percent of American households paid more in payroll taxes than income taxes.

One egregious failing of the present system is its effect on minorities with shorter life spans than the white majority. For black men age 20, only some 65 percent can be expected to survive to age 65. Thus, one of every three black youths will pay for retirement benefits they will never collect. No one intends this; and with time the gap may close. But it is not closed now. And because Social Security provides no property rights to its contributors—the Supreme Court has twice so ruled—a worker could easily work forty years then die and own not a penny of the contributions he has made for retirement benefits he will never collect. There are, to be sure, survivors and dependents benefits, but many workers die before eligibility for these is established. Disability insurance was added during the Eisenhower Administration so that workers are covered during their working years. But far too many never receive any retirement benefits and leave no estate.

*Everyone should be a part owner in the American dream.*

Similarly, the present Social Security program can prove unjust to women, especially divorced women who too often share nothing of the benefits acquired by a previous spouse. It is time we addressed this matter. There are a number of legitimate approaches that simply need to be worked out, with the plain objective of equal treatment.

As the early administrators of Social Security anticipated—and very much hoped for—the program steadily evolved. . . .

## Individual Accounts Emerge as an Alternative

In the fall of 1997, the Clinton Administration began to analyze proposals to create a system of individual retirement accounts, either as part of Social Security or outside of it. By early 1998, working groups were formed within Treasury and other departments to study issues related to such proposals.

A primary issue was how a feasible system of accounts could be administered and what would be the associated costs. In the spring of 1999 the Treasury had contracted a study by the State Street Bank entitled, "Administrative Challenges Confronting Social Security Reform." The sum of it was that the task was feasible—the Thrift Savings Accounts were already in place—and the cost modest. Accenture (formerly known as Andersen Consulting) produced similar findings. In 1998 and 1999 a range of similar measures were introduced in Congress.

None were enacted, but there was now a striking new item on the national agenda.

In the course of the Republican presidential primary campaign of 2000, then-Governor George W. Bush gave a major address on Social Security, proclaiming it "the single most successful government program in American history . . . a defining American promise." He went on to discuss Personal Retirement Accounts that would, in the words of a Democratic Senator, "take the system to its 'logical completion.'" Then-Governor Bush envisioned a program that would "give people the security of ownership," the opportunity "to build wealth, which they will use for their own retirement and pass on to their children." He cited a range of legislators, Republican and Democrat, who shared this general view, including Senator Bob Kerrey, who had recently stated: "It's very important, especially for those of us who have already accumulated wealth, to write laws to enable other people to accumulate it." Governor Bush then added:

> Ownership in our society should not be an exclusive club. Independence should not be a gated community. Everyone should be a part owner in the American dream.

In his address, then-Governor Bush insisted that "personal accounts are not a substitute for Social Security," but a supplement, a logical completion. He proposed several measures necessary to ensure the long-term fiscal viability of Social Security itself. Among them was the following:

> Reform should include personal retirement accounts for young people—an element of all the major bipartisan plans. The idea works very simply. A young worker can take some portion of his or her payroll tax and put it in a fund that invests in stocks and bonds. We will establish basic standards of safety and soundness, so that investments are only in steady, reliable funds. There will be no fly-by-night speculators or day trading. And money in this account could only be used for retirement, or passed along as an inheritance.

## There Are Many Options for Personal Accounts

Personal retirement accounts within Social Security could be designed and financed in a number of ways, some of which are analyzed by the Commission in detail. . . . To illustrate the power of personal accounts, however, let us offer the following example. This approach would establish an opportunity for all people with earnings to set up a personal retirement account, on a voluntary basis. These accounts could be financed by the individual worker voluntarily adding one percent of his pay on top of the present 6.2 percent employee share of the Social Security payroll tax. The Federal government could match the employee's contribution with a matching one percent of salary, drawn from general revenues. The result would be retirement savings accounts for all participating American workers and their families, which might or might not interact directly with the Social Security system, depending on design choices. . . . The cost to the Federal government would be approximately $40 billion per year, depending on rates of participation. The magic of compound interest now commences to work its wonders.

To illustrate what a participant might anticipate from setting aside one percent of his or her pay, matched with the government's one percent, we can forecast the situation of a "scaled medium earner" entering the workforce at age 21 and retiring at age 65 in the year 2052. Assume a portfolio choice—there should be choices—roughly that of the current Thrift Savings Plan: 50 percent corporate equity. 30 percent corporate bonds, and 20 percent U.S. Treasury bonds. Real yields are assumed to be 6.5 percent for equities, 3.5 percent for corporate bonds, and 3 percent for Treasury bonds. Also assume that this worker pays 0.3 percent of his account assets for annual administrative costs. At retirement, she or he will have an expected portfolio worth $523,000 ($101,000 in constant 2001 dollars). A two-earner family could easily have an expected net "cash" worth of $1 million.

As the Commission's interim report has shown, Social Security is in need of an overhaul. The system is not sustainable as currently structured. . . .

Regardless of how policymakers come to terms with the underlying sustainability issues, however, one thing is clear to us: the time to include personal accounts in such action has, indeed, arrived. The details of such accounts are negotiable, but their need is clear. The time for our elected officials to begin that discussion . . . is now.

# 5

# Privatizing Social Security Is a Bad Idea

## Catherine Hill

*Catherine Hill is a study director at the Institute for Women's Policy Research (IWPR), a nonprofit research organization dedicated to economic and social policy issues affecting women and families.*

Social Security is a government-run program that pays retirement benefits to seniors. Although many people claim the program is facing a severe financial crisis and they point to privatization as a way to "save" Social Security, the problems are not as bad as they seem. Privatizing Social Security by allowing seniors to invest some of the money in the stock market or bonds would be extremely expensive because of the transition and administrative costs that would be necessary to develop the new system. It is also too risky to encourage so much investment in the stock market because it is volatile. People could end up losing their money and have to rely on government programs to survive. Women would be especially hard hit by such a policy change because they typically live longer than men and are more likely to rely on Social Security as their only source of income.

You've probably heard the rumor that Social Security won't be there for you when you retire. And you've also probably heard that [President] George Bush promised to "save" Social Security by allowing individuals to divert [up to 6%] of their wages (or earnings) into individual accounts. Stocks generally have higher returns than government bonds, so setting up individual accounts that take advantage of these higher returns should mean more money when you retire. Right? Wrong. In fact, privatizing Social Security will mean less income in retirement for almost all American workers, and it will be particularly damaging for women.

## How Social Security Works

Since 1935, Social Security has been America's most successful social program, currently providing income to 48 million retired and disabled Americans and their families. More than three-fifths of retired households depend on Social Security for more than half of their income. For 25% of older women living alone, it is their only source of income. Without Social Security, half of [the] elderly people in the United States would be poor (meaning that an elderly couple would have an income under $10,000 annually and an elderly individual would have less than $8,000 to live on).

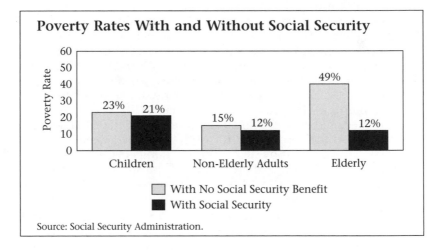

Source: Social Security Administration.

A payroll tax supplies the revenue for Social Security. The tax is currently 12.4% on wages up to $72,600 and is split between employers and employees (6.2% each) with self-employed people paying the full tax themselves. (Workers also pay 1.45% of wages or earnings for Medicare.) Note that, because most of the payroll revenues are immediately used to pay benefits, diverting "only" 2% of wages means a one-sixth reduction in the money available to pay benefits.

Social Security benefits are available to all workers and their families regardless of income. For this reason, Social Security has historically enjoyed a stronger base of political support than programs that provide benefits only to those who can document poverty, such as Supplemental Security Income (SSI). The average monthly check for a retired worker is $825 with a maximum benefit of $1,373 for a worker with a consistently high salary over a full career (35 years). While no one gets rich from Social Security, it is an important source of income for almost all retired and disabled Americans.

## Why There Isn't a Financial Crisis

Every year the Social Security Trustees forecast the long-term revenues and expenditures for the program over the next 75 years, based on demographic and economic assumptions. In the early 1980s, the Trustees forecasted a financial shortfall (misreported in the press as a "crisis"). In response, Congress increased the payroll tax rate slightly and increased the retirement age (eligibility for full Social Security benefits) from 65 to 67. These changes generated billions of dollars in surpluses for Social Security, which were placed in the Social Security Trust Fund (currently valued at a little more than $896 billion). The Trust Fund earns interest, and both principal and interest can be used to supplement payroll tax revenue during the peak Baby Boom retirement years. In 1991, the Trustees decided to use more pessimistic assumptions about future economic growth, resulting in the prediction that Social Security would not be able to pay full benefits after 2034. Strong economic performance in the last few years has resulted in a lengthening of the projected solvency to 2037. If the economy does not slow down as much as predicted, and payroll tax revenues continue to grow at a healthy rate, Social Security has no long-term solvency problem. In any case, if the economy does slow down, the Social Security program is well-positioned to continue paying full benefits for at least another thirty-seven years. After 2037, Social Security can provide three-quarters of promised benefits, and with small policy changes, Social Security can continue to pay full benefits indefinitely.

## The Politics Behind Privatization

Privatizing Social Security would be the largest undertaking in the history of the U.S. financial-services industry. It could also be the most profitable, and Wall Street knows it. For nearly two decades, Wall Street and its conservative think tanks have been cultivating the public's fear that Social Security is "going bankrupt." As Jesse Jackson and other progressive leaders have noted, financial firms such as Morgan Stanley, Quick & Reilly, Inc., and State Street Boston Corporation have given millions of dollars to conservative groups like the Cato Institute to push privatizing Social Security. However, with the facts so squarely mounted against them, the movement appeared to lose momentum, and for a while, it looked like the campaign to privatize Social Security had run its course. Activists breathed a sigh of relief and went about tackling other issues. However, [in 2000], privatizers got a second wind when Presidential candidate George Bush pledged to "partially privatize" Social Security by diverting 2% of the payroll tax (a little less than a sixth of the program's revenue) into individual accounts. [More recent Bush administration plans suggest diverting 6%.] The fight is on and the privatizers have come out swinging.

## Why Privatizing Social Security Is a Bad Idea

There are four major hidden flaws of privatizing Social Security: the enormous transition from a "pay as you go" to a prefunded system, the costs associated with purchasing equivalent life and disability coverage (or maintaining the current disability and life insurance program in the context of a 16% cut in revenue), market risk, and higher administrative costs.

• *Transition Costs.* Privatizers face a costly transition period lasting 40–70 years. If pre-funded individual accounts were to be adopted, the generations living through the transition would have to pay for two systems at once, saving for their own retirement while paying for the Social Security benefits of their parents and grandparents.

• *Replacing Disability and Life Insurance.* A sleight of hand used by many privatizers is to compare "returns" from Social Security—a social insurance and retirement program—to returns from private savings that provide only retirement benefits. Social Security taxes pay for disability and life insurance as well as retirement benefits. The program provides life and disability insurance to American workers and their families at an estimated value of a $230,000 disability policy and a $354,000 life-insurance policy for a typical worker. Privatizers argue that individuals can purchase disability and life insurance from pri-

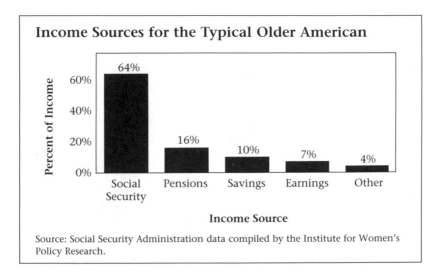

**Income Sources for the Typical Older American**

Source: Social Security Administration data compiled by the Institute for Women's Policy Research.

vate insurance firms. However, evidence from other countries' experiments with privatization suggests that insurance similar to Social Security would be costly. For people with pre-existing conditions, private disability and life insurance may not be available at any price.

• *Overly Optimistic Returns on Stocks.* Another problem with privatization is the assumption that the stock market will perform as well in the coming decades as it has in the recent past—a risky assumption. In fact, many economists believe that the stock market may be at a peak, and many stocks may be overvalued. Privatizers can't have it both ways—either the economy will be strong and the solvency problem projected for the current system won't materialize, or the economy will slow and the rate of return on stocks will drop, lowering the balances of individual accounts. Even if the stock market does well on average, individual accounts mean that there would be winners and losers. People who have greater knowledge and more money to invest will get higher returns than others. For low earners, who have less to invest and are less able to take risks, attaining average rates of return is unlikely. People who are unlucky or unwise could end up losing most or all of their money, placing additional burdens on SSI and other government programs that provide some safety net to poor people.

• *Administrative Costs.* Another problem with the privatizers' arithmetic is the failure to account for administrative costs. It costs a lot more to administer 150 million individual accounts than a single centralized system like Social Security. Experts conservatively estimate that it would cost about $25–$50 per participant per year to administer on top of the current system, which costs about $16 per person. Even small increases in management costs that are assessed monthly or annually can result in a large loss of value over one's lifetime. For example, if the costs of operating a system of individual accounts were 1% of account balances each year (a conservative estimate of the administrative costs of a 401(k) plan), these costs would consume approximately 20% of funds in personal accounts over a 40-year career, in addition to (not instead of) the current costs for administering Social Security. For lower income workers who have smaller accounts, administrative costs would absorb a greater percentage of their total value.

## Why Privatizing Social Security Would Hurt Women

Social Security is important for women because older women enter retirement with fewer economic resources than men. For example, in 1998, older women had a higher poverty rate (12.8%) than older men (7.2%). Women of color are particularly at risk for poverty in their old age. Overall, there is a substantial gender gap in all sources of retirement income including Social Security, pensions, savings, and post-retirement employment. The greatest disparity lies in accumulated pension wealth and savings, with Social Security credits partially compensating for this gap.

Furthermore, the Social Security system is progressive. Those with lower incomes have a higher proportion of their earnings replaced, which is valuable for women since they tend to earn less than men do. Income inequality would be further exacerbated in a privatized system because women investors, who have fewer resources, would get a lower yield on their investment as they would (appropriately) avoid risk.

Another important component of Social Security for women is the spousal benefit available to wives (or husbands) or widows (or widowers) who earned significantly less than their spouses. A married person is eligible for the larger of either 100% of his or her own retired worker benefit or 50% of his or her spouse's retired worker benefit. Women (or men) divorced after ten years of marriage can claim spousal benefits, even if their former partner remarries. Women make up the vast majority of recipients using the spousal benefit provision.

In 1997, 13% of women beneficiaries claimed spousal benefits compared with 2% of men. While the spousal benefit is an imperfect acknowledgement of unpaid care-giving, it is preferable to a system of individual accounts which allocates no monetary reward for child-rearing or elder care.

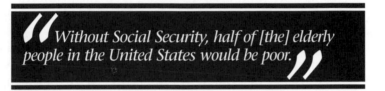

*Without Social Security, half of [the] elderly people in the United States would be poor.*

Social Security's "gender neutral" benefits mean that women don't have to pay more to compensate for their longer life expectancies—another advantage that would be lost in privatization.

The fact that Social Security provides an inflation-adjusted benefit guaranteed for life is particularly important to older women (who live on average three years longer than men).

Another aspect of Social Security that is especially valuable to women is the life and disability insurance, which includes benefits to spouses caring for children under 16 if the worker retires, becomes disabled, or dies. As women provide the bulk of care-giving in our society (for the elderly and disabled as well as for children), any shortcomings in disability and life insurance caused by privatization would have a special adverse impact on women.

## Social Security Can Do Better

Having looked at the serious drawbacks of privatizing Social Security, we can return to the real issues facing Social Security. Certainly, it is true that people are living longer and that prudent financial planning dictates that the government should maintain adequate reserves. To the extent there are long-term solvency concerns, there are a number of ways to increase revenue into Social Security. For example, the cap on the earnings subject to the payroll tax could be lifted, meaning that everyone—even those who make six or seven figures—would pay the same payroll tax rate. Another (no doubt unpopular) approach would be to allow all Social Security benefits to be taxed as income and use these revenues for benefits. Investing a portion of the Trust Fund in higher-yield public or private securities is another option. This recommendation differs from proposals that privatize Social Security through individual accounts because investments would be made by a central, independent organization, sharing risk across the entire system and holding down administrative costs. Moreover, only a small portion of the Social Security fund reserves would be dedicated to this alternative investment strategy, thus limiting the system's overall exposure to risk.

It is also true that Americans, especially low- and moderate-income Americans, don't save enough for retirement. Even with generous tax deferment for pensions, it is increasingly clear that private pension plans will never cover the entire workforce. More than two decades after the Employee Retirement Income Security Act (ERISA), more than half of American workers are not covered by a pension plan. The economic situation for older women is particularly bleak. Among the elderly, women are only about half as likely as men to receive income from private pensions (including income from a spouse's pension), and those who do receive pension benefits that are only about half as large as men's benefits. For example, in 1996, pension income for women averaged $3,679, compared with $6,442 for men.

Differences in access to pensions represent a significant gap in federal resources. Because pension funds' earnings are not taxed, because employer contributions to pensions are considered tax-deductible business expenses, and because employees are not taxed until they retire (and begin drawing a pension), there is a significant tax advantage for pension holders. For example, in 1999, the Office of Management and Budget estimated that the federal government lost $84 billion in tax revenue. Thus, unequal access to pensions means that these tax favors are also unequally distributed. . . .

The safety net for the poorest elderly and disabled people is dropping lower and lower as means-tested programs, such as SSI, fail to keep pace with a growing economy. Under constant pressure to protect Social Security from Wall Street's wrecking ball, advocacy groups and politicians have shied away from increasing benefits for anyone. However, there is ample evidence that such improvements are needed—particularly for disabled people and older women not living with men, who are at high risk for poverty.

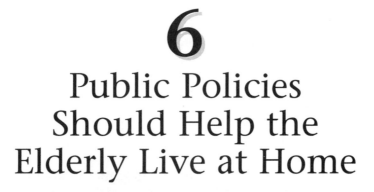

# 6

# Public Policies Should Help the Elderly Live at Home

## National Association of Area Agencies on Aging

*The National Association of Area Agencies on Aging (N4A) is the umbrella organization for the 655 area agencies on aging in the United States. N4A's primary mission is to help older people and those with disabilities live with dignity in their homes and communities for as long as possible.*

Aging adults overwhelmingly want to remain in their own homes as opposed to living in a nursing home or board and care center. In a 1999 ruling known as the *Olmstead* decision, the U.S. Supreme Court agreed that elderly and disabled people should be able to live in the community in the least restrictive setting possible. However, even though home care is better for seniors and cheaper than nursing homes, current public policies still favor institutionalization of the elderly. National public policies should be changed to support home care and community-based services in order to best address the medical, social, and environmental needs of the old.

As individuals age, and chronic conditions increase, the need for long-term care services grows. Long-term care refers to a broad range of services, paid and unpaid and provided in a variety of settings, for persons who need assistance with daily activities due to a physical or mental limitation. The availability of formal or informal support and services, an individual's needs and preferences and the ability to finance needed services all play a part in determining the setting in which an individual will receive long-term care services. According to a recent General Accounting Office (GAO) report, of the almost six million adults age 65 and over with long-term care needs, only 20 percent receive care services in a nursing home or other institutional setting, with the remaining 80 percent receiving assistance at home and in the community. Home and community-based care, which allows individuals to maintain their independence and age with dignity in the comfort of their own homes, in familiar neighborhoods and communities, is overwhelmingly the preferred choice of older adults, as well as individuals with disabilities.

Our federal policies do not adequately recognize that the most cost-effective form of long-term care is provided through home and community-based services. These services are currently provided through a fragmented and inconsistent array of federal, state, local, and private support services paid for through public and private financing. Moreover, despite the substantial role that family caregivers play in providing long-term care, the United States lacks a coherent set of policies to assist informal caregivers. Demographic changes, the aging of the 77 million baby-boomers, and increasing longevity will intensify current delivery and financing difficulties.

## *Olmstead* Decision Calls for Least Restrictive Setting

The 1999 Supreme Court *Olmstead v. L.C.* decision has accelerated the shift of national policy toward home and community-based services. In *Olmstead*, the Court ruled that the unnecessary segregation of individuals in long-term care facilities constitutes discrimination under the Americans with Disabilities Act (ADA). States are required, when it is appropriate and reasonable to do so, to serve individuals with disabilities in community settings rather than in institutions. The Court directed each state to develop a comprehensive, effective working plan to place qualified individuals in less restrictive settings and to assure that people come off waiting lists at a reasonable pace.

*Olmstead* affects those at risk of institutionalization as well as those currently institutionalized. Therefore, any reform efforts brought on by the decision must involve changes not only to the long-term provision of public health services (primarily Medicaid) but also to housing, transportation and other fundamental support services that are essential to fully integrate individuals with disabilities into least restrictive settings.

## Community-Based Case System Is Badly Needed

A comprehensive national policy that shifts the focus *and* funding of long-term care to community-based services is essential to meet the needs and address the desires of America's aging population. Independence, dignity and choice are strongly held values by all Americans, and individuals with physical or cognitive limitations and impairments are no exception. By shifting national policies toward home and community-based services, the quality of life of older adults will improve, taxpayers will be spared the cost of premature and expensive institutional care, and our nation's core values will be honored.

> *A comprehensive national policy that shifts the focus* and *funding of long-term care to community-based services is essential.*

A sound home and community-based system of long-term care provides a coordinated and broad range of services that address the medical, social and environmental needs of the individual. . . . The following principles must be adhered to for a home and community-based system to best meet the needs of those it serves, including the not-too-distant future needs of the baby boomer generation.

*Reform Medicaid.* Medicaid, the largest public program financing long-term care, has an inherent bias toward institutionalization. Congress established the home and community-based service waiver in 1981 to attempt to reduce this bias. The Medicaid waiver program gives states the option to apply for waivers to fund home and community-based services for people who meet Medicaid eligibility requirements for nursing home care. A recent study by the Assistant Secretary for Planning and Evaluation with the U.S. Department of Health and Human Services found that average spending on the aged and disabled under the Medicaid home and community-based waiver saved money—providing for an individual under the waiver program

52

costs $5,820 a year compared to $29,112 for nursing home care. Even so, nursing home care remains a basic service under Medicaid, while states still face a burdensome waiver process to offer home and community-based services.

> *By shifting national priorities toward home and community-based services, the quality of life of older adults will improve.*

*Build Upon the Successes of the Older Americans Act.* The Older Americans Act (OAA) has been the foundation of services for older adults throughout the country since its enactment in 1965 and forms the nucleus of a national system of home and community-based services. OAA funds, and the services they make possible, are augmented by leveraging state and local government funding, as well as private sector, foundation, participant and volunteer contributions. OAA funding has not kept pace with inflation or the growing population of individuals eligible for services. Significant increases in federal appropriations are crucial to assure the availability of services and programs that enhance the ability of older Americans to live with maximum independence.

*Enhance Support for Family Caregivers.* The majority of people of all ages with chronic disabling conditions rely on family members or friends as their primary source of care. Nearly one out of every four households (23 percent or 22.4 million households) is involved in caregiving to persons age 50 or older. Among older adults with long-term care needs, nearly 95 percent receive some or all of their care from informal caregivers who often suffer emotional, physical and financial hardships as a result of caregiving. Furthermore, cultural and demographic changes are reducing the pool of available caregivers just as the baby boomer generation approaches retirement age. The National Family Caregiver Support Program, enacted in 2000 as part of the Older Americans Act reauthorization, and numerous state programs provide support services for caregivers, but current federal funding is insufficient to meet caregiver needs.

*Link Affordable Housing with Needed Support Services.* Housing security is critical to the health and well being of older adults. The home and community-based system will not succeed without the provision of affordable and accessible housing for older adults. Greater coordination needs to occur between housing and service providers to guarantee that support services, such as meals, personal assistance and housekeeping, as well as health services, are readily available and easily obtainable. While policy initiatives are underway to increase existing assisted living facilities stock, convert existing public housing into accessible housing, and provide increased coordination of support and housing services, progress has been slow and more commitment to these efforts by policymakers is needed.

*Develop Systems to Help Older Adults Retain Mobility.* Mobility is essential for an individual to live at home and in the community. Transportation provides necessary access to medical care, shopping for daily essentials and the ability to participate in cultural, recreational and religious activities. Feelings of isolation and loss have been reported among older adults who can no longer use personal automobiles. Public policy must focus on the provision of safe, reliable and convenient alternative means of transportation for those for whom driving is no longer an option, as well as on efforts to help older adults retain their licenses and cars for as long as possible.

> *Medicaid, the largest public program financing long-term care, has an inherent bias toward institutionalization.*

*Design Responsive Mental Health Services.* Good mental health is fundamental to the well being of older adults and has a major impact on quality of life and optimal functioning. Yet, as the U.S. Surgeon General's 1999 report on mental health points out, too many older adults struggle with mental disorders that compromise their ability to participate fully in life. Older adults underutilize mental health services, for both social and systemic reasons, and care professionals and social services personnel frequently fail to recognize the signs and symptoms of mental illness. Service gaps, lack of collaboration among service agencies, and shortages of trained personnel also contribute to a poorly functioning mental health service system. Policymakers must work toward resolving current challenges in the design and delivery of mental health services that affect quality of life for the older population.

*Expand Nutrition and Wellness Programs.* Good nutrition and daily physical activity both play important roles in preventing or forestalling the onset of chronic conditions as well as reducing the effects of existing conditions. Nutrition programs such as congregate and home-delivered meals, provided through the Older Americans Act and other government programs, not only improve participants' dietary intake but also provide a social outlet for older adults at risk of isolation. Unfortunately, long waiting lists for these meals programs exist throughout the country. And while fewer structured programs exist to promote physical activity, the social, economic and health benefits of daily exercise must be recognized. Greater emphasis needs to be placed on the development and expansion of programs that promote sound nutrition and increased physical activity at the federal, state and local level.

*Increase Efforts to Prevent Elder Abuse and Neglect.* The dependence on others for care and assistance whether at home or in a facility leaves older adults, especially the most frail, vulnerable to abuse, neglect and exploitation. Adult protective services are designed to reduce the incidence of abuse and neglect and are essential to making it possible for older adults to remain safely in their homes and communities. Many older adult victims do not report abuse and many cases are not prosecuted. Staffing shortages, poor training and heavy caseloads contribute to unsatisfactory protective services. Greater outreach and educational efforts and increased collaboration among service providers at the federal, state and local level are important measures that can be taken to prevent and decrease all types of elder abuse.

*Collaborate on Solutions to Workforce Shortages.* At a time when an increasing percentage of the population needs direct care services, our nation is facing a serious shortage of workers in this industry. Paraprofessional personnel shortages can be attributed to, among other things, low pay, inadequate employee benefits including lack of health insurance, insufficient training and minimal chance for career advancement. Moreover, health care agencies have a hard time maintaining employees due primarily to poor reimbursement rates from both public (Medicare, Medicaid) and private providers. Furthermore, the care that is provided by these workers is undervalued by society. Policymakers need to work collaboratively with workers unions, service providers and consumers to recruit and retain a stable, reliable workforce.

# 7

# The Government Must Increase Funding for Alzheimer's Research and Care

## Stephen McConnell

*Stephen McConnell is senior vice president of advocacy and public policy for the Alzheimer's Association, a nonprofit organization dedicated to eradicating Alzheimer's disease.*

Alzheimer's disease may be the biggest epidemic of the twenty-first century. An estimated 4.5 million Americans currently have Alzheimer's, a progressive disease that dramatically impairs memory and is ultimately fatal. Over the next fifty years that number is expected to reach 16 million as the baby boom generation ages. The financial cost of Alzheimer's is staggering, and caring for those who have the disease is extremely demanding. The federal government should increase funding for Alzheimer's research in order to find a cure or a way to prevent Alzheimer's and to improve the lives of those who already have the disease.

*Editor's Note: Stephen McConnell presented the following testimony to the U.S. Senate Special Committee on Aging on April 27, 2004.*

The growing epidemic of Alzheimer's disease is generating catastrophic human and economic costs to American society and to societies around the world. The goal of the Alzheimer's

Stephen McConnell, testimony before the U.S. Senate Special Committee on Aging, Washington, DC, April 27, 2004.

Association, working in partnership with government and private industry, is to eradicate this disease. Through these combined efforts of the Association, National Institutes of Health, and the pharmaceutical industry, advances in medical treatment have surged forward in recent years.

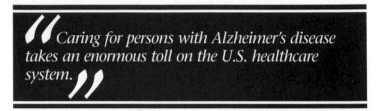

*Caring for persons with Alzheimer's disease takes an enormous toll on the U.S. healthcare system.*

In the meantime, we must improve diagnosis, treatment and care; support family caregivers; address human resource challenges in the delivery of health care services; and improve care in facilities, at home, and in communities, whether rural, suburban or urban. We must do this in cost-effective ways that enhance quality of life for individuals, families and caregivers.

These are no small challenges, but technology provides enormous opportunities for addressing them. The Alzheimer's Association has assumed a leadership role by investing significant resources in exploring these technologies. . . . In addition, the Alzheimer's Association recently announced that more than 150 local, state and national organizations representing more than 50 million Americans have come together to form the "Coalition of Hope"—the largest coalition ever organized to support increased funding for research to find new treatments to help those with Alzheimer's disease. . . .

## Federal Government Should Play a Role

While much of the developmental work in technology is being carried out by private sector organizations, the Alzheimer's Association believes there is a definite role for the federal government. In addition to continued oversight, a key role is to bring stakeholders together in order to draw attention to the issues and give impetus to developmental efforts. A national commission on technology and aging, with special emphasis on those with cognitive impairment, should be created to focus public and private attention and resources on addressing these issues. A series of additional hearings should be convened to provide oversight on progress, to stimulate interest among various stakeholders, and to identify policy impediments to implementation of technological solutions.

Other roles for the federal government include supporting research on assistive technology in partnership with private industry and voluntary health agencies like the Alzheimer's Association. In addition, emphasis should be placed on continuing and increasing federal funding for Alzheimer's disease research to maintain the momentum of advanced understanding of the causes and potential treatments of the disease while also seeking to find solutions for improving the care of those already diagnosed with the disease.

## The Growing Alzheimer's Epidemic

The challenges posed by Alzheimer's disease affect this country at a personal, an economic, and a societal level. An estimated 4.5 million Americans currently have Alzheimer's disease. Increasing age is the greatest risk factor for Alzheimer's. One in ten individuals over age 65 and nearly half over 85 are affected. The number of Americans with Alzheimer's will continue to grow as our population ages and life expectancy rates soar. By 2050, Alzheimer's could affect anywhere from 11.3 million to 16 million people.

## Alzheimer's Costs Are Skyrocketing

Caring for persons with Alzheimer's disease takes an enormous toll on the U.S. healthcare system. At any particular time, approximately 20 percent (1.1 million) of persons with Alzheimer's are in nursing homes and between five and ten percent (450,000–600,000) are in assisted living facilities. By 2010, Medicare costs for beneficiaries with Alzheimer's are expected to increase nearly 55 percent, from $31.9 billion in 2000 to $49.3 billion and Medicaid expenditures on residential dementia care will increase 80 percent, from $18.2 billion to $33 billion. Nearly half (49 percent) of Medicare beneficiaries who have Alzheimer's disease also receive Medicaid. The average annual cost of Alzheimer care in a nursing home is $64,000.

Medicaid pays nearly half of the total nursing home bill and helps two out of three residents pay for their care. Alzheimer's disease costs American business $61 billion annually, $36.5 billion of which is caused by the lost productivity of employees who are caregivers. Utilizing assistive technologies to prolong a person's ability to live independently, thus reducing the need for expensive institutional care, has the potential to save billions of dollars in Medicare and Medicaid spending, as well as family budgets.

## Caregiving Is Demanding Work

Caring for persons with Alzheimer's also places a heavy burden on the families and friends of those with the disease. Alzheimer caregiving is intense, hard, and exhausting work. Seventy percent of people with Alzheimer's live at home, where family and friends provide the majority of their care. Alzheimer caregivers devote more time to the day-to-day tasks of caring and they provide help with greater numbers of activities of daily living (including incontinence, one of the biggest challenges of caregiving). One in eight Alzheimer caregivers becomes ill or injured as a direct result of caregiving and one in three uses medications for problems related to caregiving.

Older caregivers are three times more likely to become clinically depressed than others in their age group and one study found that elderly spouses strained by caregiving were 63 percent more likely to die during a four-year period than other spouses their age. Assistive devices that allow individuals with cognitive impairments to complete activities of daily living with less dependence on their caregivers is one area in which technology may help alleviate some of the fatigue and "caregiver burnout" faced by loved ones of individuals with Alzheimer's disease.

> *Utilizing assistive technologies to prolong a person's ability to live independently, thus reducing the need for expensive institutional care, has the potential to save billions of dollars.*

The caregiving challenges presented by Alzheimer's disease extend to the long term care workforce as well. Today more than 1 million nursing assistants provide as much as 90 percent of hands-on care in nursing homes and other settings. The Bureau of Labor Statistics estimates that by 2006, personal home and care aides are projected to be the fourth-fastest growing occupation, with a dramatic 84.7 percent growth rate expected. Despite the growth in the industry and the increased demand for talented workers, there is a long term care workforce crisis. National long term care staff turnover rates are at an alarming 94 percent annually.

## Better Training Is Needed

Numerous issues contribute to this crisis including insufficient staff, low wages, inadequate benefits, lack of dementia-specific training, little or no job recognition and few career advancement opportunities. Staffing shortages affect the overall quality of care to residents and contribute directly to staff turnover. One of the most important steps toward improving the quality of care is better training. Certified Nursing Assistants surveyed in a 1999 Iowa Caregiver's Association report indicated that their work was increasingly demanding and complex and that they needed more training and orientation. Respondents specifically mentioned the importance of Alzheimer's training and understanding behaviors related to dementia. With up to 16 million people expected to develop Alzheimer's disease by the middle of the 21st century, nearly all of whom will eventually require total care, a solution to the workforce crisis must be found immediately. Technology that can be used to provide ongoing, interactive training for staff in long term care facilities is one part of the solution to the broader workforce problem.

## Symptoms and Signs of Alzheimer's

Individuals living with Alzheimer's disease face challenges at all stages of the disease. Common symptoms at the beginning and moderate stages are impaired memory, judgment, and reasoning ability. As Alzheimer's progresses, individuals with the disease may lose the ability to manage their own health care, may not be able to follow medication instructions, and may need frequent cueing or reminders when completing routine tasks. All are likely at some point in the disease process to require 24-hour supervision and assistance. Individuals with Alzheimer's may also experience difficult or challenging behavior problems that lead to violent episodes, an issue explored by this committee in a hearing just last month [March 2004]. Several population-based studies have found that upwards of 90 percent of people with dementia develop one or more psychiatric and related behavioral problems. Wandering is another common and potentially life-threatening behavior associated with Alzheimer's disease. Studies report wandering in 4 to 26 percent of nursing home residents with dementia and in up to 59 percent of community-residing individuals suffering from the disease. Utilizing existing technology, such as electronic monitoring devices, may provide solutions to the everyday challenges faced by individuals with Alzheimer's disease.

## Technology Can Play a Key Role in Care

Technological innovations have enormous potential to address some of the challenges posed by Alzheimer's disease. Through our partnership with The Center for Aging Services Technologies (CAST), the Alzheimer's Association is working to identify how technology can improve Alzheimer's care and services. CAST has identified four areas where technology might improve aging services—providing ways to improve independence and allow people to remain independent longer (enabling); addressing the human resources and productivity issues of aging services providers (operational); improving the connections between individuals and their families and social support networks (connective); and dealing with geographic barriers to good care (telemedicine). These focus areas coincide with key priority areas for Alzheimer's care.

> *With up to 16 million people expected to develop Alzheimer's disease by the middle of the 21st century, nearly all of whom will eventually require total care, a solution to the workforce crisis must be found immediately.*

An example of enabling technology that may help prolong independent living is a "Smart House" that includes features such as stoves with automatic cutoff devices and kitchen heat sensors to prevent fires. "Smart Houses" may also include devices that cue and remind individuals with Alzheimer's disease to take medications or help them locate lost possessions. In addition, Artificial Intelligence is being tested to help individuals with Alzheimer's disease complete activities of daily living with less dependence on their caregivers.

Promoting safety is another major concern of the Alzheimer's Association. A wide variety of electronic tracking devices are currently available to monitor, track and locate individuals with Aizheimer's disease who wander. . . .

Telemedicine has the potential to reduce geographic barriers to good care. Telehealth and telemedicine technologies are being assessed for possible use in providing supervision (including monitoring sleep and eating patterns and medication compliance/accuracy) of individuals with Alzheimer's who live alone.

## Success Requires a Team Effort

Developing, testing and measuring the viability and feasibility of various technologies to improve care and promote healthy aging requires collaboration among technology companies, researchers, service providers and advocacy organizations. Meeting the distinct needs of the aging population, particularly those with Alzheimer's disease, will require a complex, multidimensional approach. . . .

In recent years, while advances in treatments for brief symptomatic relief have surged forward, progress in improving services and technologies for routine care of people with prolonged disability and loss of independent functioning have lagged behind. Delaying and eventually preventing cognitive impairments could have far greater significance for the economics of health and well being than providing short-term, symptomatic relief. . . .

## Public Policy Issues

There are a variety of public policy aspects, especially around reimbursement and regulatory issues, that may influence the broader development and adoption of assistive technologies for seniors and individuals with Alzheimer's disease. For example, alternative treatment models using telemedicine to help manage care for persons with Alzheimer's disease in rural areas might be very successful, but these models are not currently reimbursable, or reimbursement is very cumbersome. Determining how to measure the practical and care outcomes of using technology, conducting additional research to assess whether technology can reduce the cost of care or increase caregiver efficiency, and promoting more widespread use of existing technology in various care settings are just a few of the challenges faced by this burgeoning field. It will be necessary for government and private industry to examine all public policies, including possible Medicare and Medicaid reimbursement, to determine the impact on the development, adoption and use of technology. . . .

## Technology Poses Challenges Too

Efforts to incorporate the use of technology more broadly in the care of persons with cognitive impairments such as Alzheimer's disease pose some unique challenges for caregivers in all settings. These challenges include:

• Adapting existing technologies so that they can be utilized by people with cognitive impairments.

• Determining the applicability of existing technologies in various Alzheimer's care settings.

• Considering the ethical issues related to use of technology, such as obtaining consent, maintaining privacy rights and preserving decision-making autonomy for individuals with cognitive impairments.

• Responding to cultural, language and ethnicity issues, both in how people will react to technology and to ensure technology is diffused into communities in ways that are culturally appropriate.

• Developing models that integrate human aspects with technology to deliver high quality care with greater efficiency.

All of these issues can be addressed, and while they address issues specific to people with cognitive impairments, they are important to everyone who will be using or be affected by technology in care settings. . . .

As was acknowledged earlier, much of the developmental work in technology is being carried out by private sector organizations the Alzheimer's Association believes the federal government can play a role in this area by:

• Creating a national commission on technology and aging, with a special emphasis on those with cognitive impairments, to focus public and private attention and resources on addressing these issues.

• Supporting research on assistive technology in partnership with private industry and voluntary health agencies like the Alzheimer's Association.

• Convening a series of additional hearings to provide over-sight on progress, to stimulate interest among various stake-holders and to identify policy impediments to implementation of technological solutions.

• Continuing and increasing federal funding for Alzheimer's disease research to maintain the momentum of advanced un-derstanding of the causes and potential treatments of the dis-ease while also seeking to find solutions for improving the care of those already diagnosed with the disease.

## Entering a New Era

We have entered a new era in the fight against Alzheimer's dis-ease. Over the last twenty years we have gone from hopeless to hopeful and are at the point where the goal of a world without Aizheimer's disease is within reach. Working collaboratively, the federal government, the scientific community, the Alz-heimer's Association and the pharmaceutical industry have made tremendous progress in the prevention, diagnosis and treatment of Alzheimer's disease. Even with the progress that has been made, we still face many challenges, especially in de-livering healthcare services and improving care for individuals with Alzheimer's disease in facilities, at home and in commu-nities. These are big challenges but technology provides enor-mous opportunities for addressing them.

The Alzheimer's Association has assumed a leadership role by investing significant resources in exploring these technologies through the creation of a Technology Workgroup, by launching with Intel Corporation the Everyday Technologies for Alz-heimer's Care consortium, and by joining the Center for Aging Services Technologies commission sponsored by the American Association of Homes & Services for the Aging. While much of the developmental work in technology is being carried out by private sector organizations, it is essential that the federal gov-ernment intervene to enable both sectors to focus more atten-tion and resources on this promising area. We are committed to working with you and all of our partner organizations to shape a future in which technology will improve the lives of people with chronic conditions like Alzheimer's disease, as well as the lives of their caregivers and families.

# 8

# The Government Must Provide Transportation Programs for Seniors Who Cannot Drive

## Larry Lipman

*Larry Lipman covers aging issues as a senior reporter with Cox News Service, a newspaper wire service.*

For most elderly people, being able to drive a car is an important part of their independence. However, many seniors continue driving longer than they safely should because they do not want to give up their freedom or because they fear imposing on family or friends to take them places. Every year, about eight hundred thousand senior citizens in the United States give up driving—but they still need to go places. More government funding is needed for transportation programs for seniors, especially because the number of nondrivers will grow so rapidly over the next thirty years.

Jane Tuttle quit driving the day a routine shopping trip turned terrifying. Alone and needing to get home, Tuttle, 81, discovered she was unable to feel the difference between the gas and brake pedals because of a medical condition that can cause numbness in the feet. She made it home that day without incident, but after 65 years of driving she gave her car keys to her son. "It's been a big shock to find myself without wheels. It's terrible. You are totally dependent," Tuttle said.

Larry Lipman, "America Facing a Crisis of Elderly Non-Drivers," Cox News Service, April 13, 2004. Copyright © 2004 by Cox Enterprises, Inc. Reproduced by permission.

Fears of isolation or loss of independence keep many elderly people behind the wheel beyond the time it's safe. But as America ages, it will inevitably face a transportation crisis for those who no longer drive.

## Country Is Not Prepared

It's a crisis for which the nation has made few preparations. Older non-drivers are reluctant to impose on friends, who often have their own driving difficulties. Walking and public transportation are usually not adequate options, and the idea of community-based transportation networks for the elderly are just starting to take root.

The problem is growing quickly. An estimated 800,000 elderly people quit driving in the United States each year. Millions more limit the time of day, the type of roads, or the distance they travel. Already, more than 7 million Americans over 65—one in five—are non-drivers, according to the U.S. Department of Transportation. . . . The average age at which elderly drivers quit is about 85, according to Daniel J. Foley, an epidemiologist at the National Institute on Aging. Currently, about 7 million Americans are 85 and older. That will increase to about 9 million by 2030, when the oldest of today's baby boomers hit their mid-80s, and will nearly triple to 19 million by 2050.

Most people can expect to live for many years after they've quit driving. A study led by Foley determined that on average, elderly women live another 10 years, and men live another seven years, after they stop driving.

## Losing Driving Privilege Is Traumatic

Public attention has been focused on making sure that elderly drivers are safe on the road, such as Florida's law this year [2004] requiring vision screening for all drivers 80 or older when they renew their license. Other efforts have been aimed at making it easier for elderly drivers to continue driving—by making road signs more visible, building separate left-turn lanes and improving car technology to make information such as directions more available. But there has been little focus on what happens when people can no longer drive.

"We have far to go in thinking what to do with these people now that we've taken their independence, their self-esteem, their self-worth and said: 'You're a danger, you can't drive any more,'" said Stella Henry, founder and director of the Vista del Sol Care Center, a long-term care facility in Culver City, Calif.

"Going grocery shopping, going to the cleaners, visiting a friend, the grandchild, or simply just getting out for a cup of bad coffee is what life is about," said Joseph Coughlin, director of the Massachusetts Institute of Technology's AgeLab.

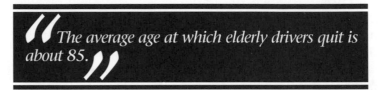

*The average age at which elderly drivers quit is about 85.*

Many former drivers become virtual prisoners in their homes, experts say. Typical is Jerry Gismondi, of Boca Raton, Fla., who quit driving two decades ago and relies on a local senior center bus to go to the center and grocery store. The 75-year-old misses going out for an evening movie or the symphony because of a lack of late-night public transportation. Taxis are too expensive, he said, and he's reluctant to ask friends. "I feel embarrassed," he said.

## Non-Drivers Experience Isolation

A recent report by the Surface Transportation Policy Project, a nonprofit coalition of groups interested in promoting safe communities and transportation alternatives, found that:

• More than half of non-drivers over 65 stay home on any given day, citing a lack of transportation options.

• Compared with elderly drivers, elderly non-drivers make 15 percent fewer doctor trips, 60 percent fewer shopping and dining trips, and 65 percent fewer trips for social, family and religious activities.

• Non-driving is more common in minority communities. While about 16 percent of elderly whites do not drive, 39 percent of older Latinos, 42 percent of blacks and 45 percent of Asian-Americans do not drive.

For many older non-drivers, options are limited. Once they give up driving, many elderly rely on family and friends to drive them. But family members may not live nearby, or may find it a strain to provide transportation in the middle of a workday. Friends may be roughly the same age as the former driver and barely able to drive themselves. Friendships might be strained by relying on another person for a ride, particularly if it involves a lengthy wait at a doctor's office for example. When that happens, an elderly person may feel "so embarrassed . . . they don't feel like they can get a ride with them again because they feel they have taken up such a big hunk of that person's time," said Jon E. Burkhardt, a senior study director at WESTAT, a Rockville, Md., research group. "Sometimes it's hard for older folks to pay back a favor like 'take me to the doctors' office,' particularly if that takes three or four hours."

## Public Transportation Poses Hardship

Experts say public transportation is not the answer. With the population shift out of the cities since World War II, more than half of America's elderly live in the suburbs, and another quarter live in rural areas, far from public transportation. Even those who do live near public transportation may be unable to use it. The same physical and mental health problems that often lead people to quit driving make it difficult for them to use public transportation. A bus stop several blocks away may be too far for an elderly person to walk, particularly in snow and ice. Waiting for a bus in the heat also may be too difficult for many. Bus steps can be difficult to navigate and bus schedules can tax the memories of those with varying degrees of dementia. More than that, experts say, people who have spent most of their lives driving are not likely to begin taking the bus in their old age. "You don't wake up at 75 and say, 'You know, I think I'll take the bus,'" Coughlin said.

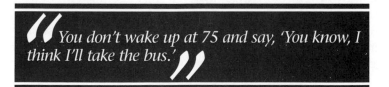

*You don't wake up at 75 and say, 'You know, I think I'll take the bus.'*

Use of public transit nationally by the elderly has been steadily declining. In 1995, the elderly used public transit for a scant 2.2 percent of their trips. By 2001, that percentage had dropped to a minuscule 1.3 percent, according to Sandra Rosenbloom, director of the Roy P. Drachman Institute for Land and Regional Development Studies at the University of Arizona in a paper written for the Brookings Institution.

## Seniors Need More Options

While most large communities have alternative transportation services beyond the fixed-route public transit lines, many of them have severe limits on when they will operate, where they will go, and who is eligible to ride. "Community services, religious groups, etc., have defined the transportation needs of the elderly as basically going to the doctor, grocery or religious activity," Coughlin said. "Real life is about more than going to the drug store and going to the doctor's office." Although more than half of elderly Americans say they walk regularly, it is often not a viable alternative to driving. And while walking, in general, is good for the health, it can be dangerous as a means of transportation. "Older people are much more endangered as pedestrians than they are as drivers or car passengers," Rosenbloom said in an interview, noting the dangers of elderly people slipping on ice, leaves or tripping over roots in the sidewalk.

Some communities have encouraged the elderly to use alternative vehicles such as motorized golf carts to get around, but Rosenbloom said not enough planning has gone into making them a viable solution, even in "planned" communities where a retail hub is surrounded by neighborhoods. She said the same problems older drivers may experience may prevent them from operating alternative vehicles.

## Funding Programs Should Be a Priority

In a few places, alternative transportation programs have been provided at the local level, but federal support for such programs is limited. The federal government has provided financial aid to private organizations such as agencies on aging, the American Red Cross and United Way to purchase vans and mini-buses to bring people to their facilities. The last six-year transportation bill, which expires this year [in 2004], authorized $456 million for the program. Both the House and Senate versions of the new bill increase that funding.

Transportation assistance for the elderly "has been a cobbled-together investment of reports, events and demonstration projects," Coughlin said. "Quite frankly, we are losing time. It takes years to change infrastructure, it takes decades to change living patterns. Even if we were to act today with a coherent policy and with a real commitment," he said. "By the time the oldest group (of boomers) reaches 75, 80 years old, unless somebody puts transportation on the agenda, we're not going to make it."

# 9

## Society Must Confront Ageism and Discrimination

### David Crary

*David Crary writes on national issues for the Associated Press, a newspaper wire service.*

Society is rife with negative images and stereotypes about aging, and seniors frequently encounter age discrimination on the job and in health care settings. Cultural attitudes about getting old play a major part in how elderly people are treated in society as well as in how seniors view themselves. Attitudes about getting old may even affect how long a person lives. Many experts agree that society must work to eliminate ageism so that old age is once again respected rather than reviled.

Greeting-card and novelty companies call them "Over the Hill" products: the 50th Birthday Coffin Gift Boxes featuring prune juice and anti-aging soap; the "Old Coot" and "Old Biddy" bobblehead dolls; the birthday cards mocking the mobility, intellect and sex drive of the no-longer-young.

Many Americans chuckle at such humor. Others see it as offensive, as one more sign of pervasive ageism in America.

It's a bias some also see in substandard conditions at nursing homes, in pension-plan cutbacks by employers, in the relative invisibility of the elderly on television shows and in advertisements.

"Daily we are witness to, or even unwitting participants in, cruel imagery, jokes, language, and attitudes directed at older people," contends Dr. Robert Butler, president of the International Longevity Center–USA and the person who coined the term "ageism" 35 years ago.

That ageism exists, in a society captivated by youth culture and taut-skinned good looks, is scarcely debatable. But as the oldest of the 77 million baby boomers approach their 60s, the elderly and their concerns will inevitably move higher on the national agenda.

## Will Ageism Get Worse or Better?

Already, there is lively debate as to whether ageism will ease or grow worse in the coming decades of boomer senior citizenship. Erdman Palmore, a professor emeritus at Duke University who has written or edited more than a dozen books on aging, counts himself—cautiously—among the optimists.

"One can say unequivocally that older people are getting smarter, richer and healthier as time goes on," Palmore said. "I've dedicated most of my life to combating ageism, and it's tempting for me to see it everywhere. . . . But I have faith that as science progresses, and reasonable people get educated about it, we will come to recognize ageism as the evil it is."

Palmore, 74, lives what he preaches—challenging the stereotypes of aging by skydiving, whitewater rafting, bicycling his age in miles each birthday. He recently got a tattoo on his shoulder, though the image he chose was the relatively discreet symbol of the American Humanist Association.

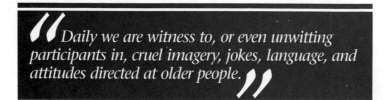

*Daily we are witness to, or even unwitting participants in, cruel imagery, jokes, language, and attitudes directed at older people.*

"What makes me mad is how aging, in our language and culture, is equated with deterioration and impairment," Palmore said. "I don't know how we're going to root that out, except by making people more aware of it."

To the extent that ageism persists, there will soon be many more potential targets. The number of Americans 65 and older is projected to double over the next three decades from 35.9

million to nearly 70 million, comprising 20 percent of the population in 2030 compared to less than 13 percent now.

The 85-and-over population is the fastest growing segment —projected to grow from 4 million in 2000 to 19 million in 2050 as part of an unprecedented surge in longevity. Americans now turning 65 will live, on average, an additional 18 years.

## Ageism May Affect Longevity

Some researchers believe that ageism, in the form of negative stereotypes, directly affects longevity. In a study published by the American Psychological Association, Yale School of Public Health professor Becca Levy and her colleagues concluded that old people with positive perceptions of aging lived an average of 7.5 years longer than those with negative images of growing older.

Levy said many Americans start developing stereotypes about the elderly during childhood, reinforce them throughout adulthood, and enter old age with attitudes toward their own age group as unfavorable as younger people's attitudes.

"It's possible to overcome the stereotypes, but they often operate without people's awareness," Levy said. "Look at all the talk about plastic surgery, Botox—the message is, 'Don't get old.'"

## Age Discrimination on the Job

For thousands of American workers, it's the same message they claim to hear on the job. The U.S. Equal Employment Opportunity Commission [EEOC] has received more than 19,000 age discrimination complaints in each of the past two years, and has helped win tens of millions of dollars in settlements.

However, attorneys say age discrimination often is hard to prove. Only about one-seventh of the EEOC age cases were settled to the complainant's benefit.

New Yorker Bill DeLong, 84, was fired three years ago from his longtime job as a waiter at a Shea Stadium restaurant, but he continues to seek out charitable volunteer assignments and still works as a waiter occasionally at special events.

"I didn't give up," he said. "A lot of my contemporaries give up too soon."

Seventy-eight-year-old Catherine Roberts stays active with New York City's Joint Public Affairs Committee for Older Adults, a coalition that encourages seniors to advocate on their own behalf on legislative and community issues.

"I don't have time to get old," said Roberts, who came to New York from Maine in 1955. "I'm too busy."

Yet despite her upbeat outlook, she resents how some of her peers are treated. "We're a culture that worships youth," she said. "Seniors are getting pushed aside. I see people in my building whose families ignore them—they fall through the cracks."

## Elders Face Ageism in Health Care

For many older people, ageism surfaces most painfully in the context of health care. A report by the Alliance for Aging Research, presented to a Senate committee last year [2003], said the elderly are less likely to receive preventive care and often lack access to doctors trained in their needs.

Only about 10 percent of U.S. medical schools require work in geriatric medicine. The American Geriatrics Society says there are only about 7,600 physicians nationwide certified as geriatric specialists—not enough to meet demand and far below the 36,000 the society says will be needed by 2030.

While the society says the best way to attract more doctors to the field is to make Medicare practice more lucrative, some experts believe that many medical students also have negative attitudes toward the elderly that should be challenged.

In one such effort, the National Institute on Aging, working with Johns Hopkins Medical School and a Baltimore museum, teamed elderly people and first-year medical students in an art program in which they drew, made collages, sang songs and shared stories. A survey showed the students gained a more positive view of seniors and of geriatrics as a possible specialty.

## Advertisers Cater to Young Market

Ageism also manifests itself in advertising. Though adults of all ages drink beer and buy cars, for example, TV and print ads for those products almost invariably feature youthful actors and models.

According to AARP, the lobbying group for people 50 and over, Americans in that age bracket account for half of all consumer spending but are targeted by just 10 percent of marketing. The dynamic is particularly potent in television, where network executives gear programming toward 18-to-34-year-olds because advertisers will pay more to reach those viewers.

"When an older person sees a product targeted to a younger person, they're willing to buy it, but young people will not buy a product targeted to an older person," said Jim Fishman, group publisher for AARP Publications.

Fishman, who oversees AARP's three magazines, predicts advertisers will increasingly tilt their messages toward older consumers as the baby boomers enter their 60s.

"By and large, the wealth that resides in the older segment of the population is disposable wealth—the kids are done with college, the mortgage is paid off," Fishman said. "This older market is huge and feeling largely ignored."

## Attitudes on Aging Are Changing

Looking ahead, Fishman foresees people of all ages, elderly included, gaining the ability to look more attractive than in the past thanks to developments ranging from Botox to fitness programs. He also expects a more deep-rooted change in society's view of aging as the 65-and-older ranks are filled with increasing numbers of computer-savvy boomers, eager for civic engagement and lifelong education programs.

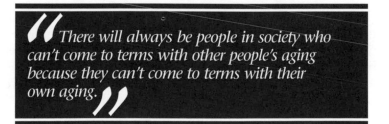

*There will always be people in society who can't come to terms with other people's aging because they can't come to terms with their own aging.*

Still, David Wolfe, whose book *Ageless Marketing* advises advertisers how to reach over-50 consumers, says ageism is likely to persist. "There will always be people in society who can't come to terms with other people's aging because they can't come to terms with their own aging," he said.

Paul Kleyman, editor of the American Society on Aging's bimonthly newspaper, has testified before Congress that ageism is common in the mass media. He tells of a magazine editor who wanted fewer stories about "prune faces," and of a Chicago talk radio station whose staff was told to screen out "old-sounding" callers.

Kleyman also detects some positive trends, including a growing number of newspapers assigning reporters to cover aging-related issues on a regular basis.

"The drive in the news industry is for younger readers, but don't just ignore the loyal older readers you have," he said. "We should be encouraging society to be receptive to a more active older generation, instead of looking at boomers as a burden that's going to drain the nation."

## The Young and the Old Compete for Resources

The short-term future of ageism may depend in large part on that question—whether or not baby boomers are viewed by younger Americans as a rival for economic resources and political clout as Society Security and Medicare costs rise.

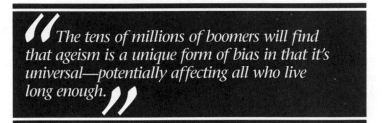

*The tens of millions of boomers will find that ageism is a unique form of bias in that it's universal—potentially affecting all who live long enough.*

"At the individual level of how people are treated, negative ageism is probably going to decline a little," said Robert Binstock, professor of aging and public policy at Case Western Reserve School of Medicine in Cleveland. "But at the societal level it's quite possible we'll see an increase in ageism, a sense of, 'Wow, what an unsustainable burden older people are going to be.'"

Bob Robinson, 88, of Aurora, Colo., a former director of services for the aging in Colorado, said he has encountered a generational gap while lobbying legislators on senior issues.

"The politicians consider that with Social Security and Medicare and the other advantages that seniors have, we're in pretty good shape," Robinson said. "It's true for a lot of us, but not for all of us. Many seniors worked for small businesses that had no retirement system."

Bobbie Sackman of New York City's Council of Senior Centers and Services agrees.

"Boomers are not all white, middle-class suburbanites," she said. "You will have the older people with greater resources, and that will in some ways change the image of aging. But you will also have those with less resources, coming from groups that already had faced discrimination, and now they will have the age thing added to the mix."

## Boomers Will Shape Society's Attitudes

John Rother, policy director for the AARP, said the boomers, by their very numbers, are bound to change the public perception of aging.

"It will be more visible," he said. "People will survive longer, in better health. . . . They'll feel the market should cater to them, the political system should cater to them, as it has their whole lives."

Whatever their political clout, the tens of millions of boomers will find that ageism is a unique form of bias in that it's universal—potentially affecting all who live long enough.

"Everyone has a vested interest in eradicating this prejudice," wrote Richard Butler, the International Longevity Center president, in a recent briefing paper. "We all aspire to live to be old, and consequently we all must work to create a society where old age is respected, if not honored, and where persons who have reached old age are not marginalized."

# 10

# The Elderly Must Be Protected from Abuse

## Robert B. Blancato

*Robert B. Blancato is the president of the National Committee to Prevent Elder Abuse (NCPEA), a nonprofit organization that promotes research, advocacy, and public awareness of elder justice issues.*

Elder abuse can take many forms: physical, emotional, financial, or sexual. Seniors may be abused by family members or others in their homes, or in institutional settings such as nursing facilities. Seniors may also be victims of self-neglect if they cannot take care of themselves adequately. Although nearly half a million seniors are abused in the United States each year, government policy about the problem has been fragmented and ineffective. A comprehensive elder abuse policy is badly needed. Such a policy should increase adult protective services, train professionals, educate the public about elder abuse, and increase the prosecution of abusers. In February 2003, Senator John Breaux (D-LA) introduced the Elder Justice Act, a comprehensive bill that will make elder abuse the priority that it should be. In September 2004 the Senate Finance Committee approved the measure 20-0.

Elder abuse is not a new issue, but it has new urgency that compels some new approaches.

Statistically, based on the National Center on Elder Abuse's collection of data from states for the year including 2000, there were a total of 470,709 reports of adult/elder abuse. This represented a 60 percent increase from 1996. In addition, an esti-

Robert B. Blancato, statement before the U.S. Senate Committee on Finance, Washington, DC, June 18, 2002.

mated 15,000 complaints of abuse and gross neglect against older victims living in nursing homes and other long-term care facilities were reported, as well as 3500 similar complaints of abuse in board and care facilities.

Yet, estimates from the Senate Special Committee on Aging suggest the number of cases could be as many as 5 million, since more than eight out of every ten cases go unreported.

The federal involvement in elder abuse spans more than 23 years beginning with Congressional hearings before the House Select Committee on Aging. Eventually, federal programs were adopted and funding was provided for elder abuse prevention programs, adult protective services, and the Long-Term Care Ombudsman Program. This history includes the funding of a National Center on Elder Abuse, a Surgeon General's Report on Family Violence including elder abuse, and a National Elder Abuse Incidence Study. More recently, . . . the first National Summit on Elder Abuse was held under the auspices of the Administration on Aging and the Department of Justice in December 2001. We also note and commend the release of the National Academy of Sciences study on Risk and Prevalence of Elder Abuse and Neglect.

The reality is the federal response to combating elder abuse and neglect has been piecemeal and ultimately inadequate, as the problem has intensified. It is said in policy that sometimes it is all about money. If that criterion were applied, the current federal commitment pales even further. Consider that the only federal program that appropriates funds specifically addressed to elder abuse, Title VII of the Older Americans Act, has national funding of less than $5 million. It is estimated that the total federal commitment being spent today on programs addressing elder abuse, neglect and financial exploitation prevention is $153 million. This is all but .08 percent of the funds currently spent on abuse prevention programs whether for children, women or the elderly. It is not surprising, but is nonetheless disturbing, as Senator [John] Breaux [D-LA] recently noted, that there is not one single person working in the federal government full time on elder abuse prevention. . . .

## Elder Justice Should Address Seven Goals

We need to move to a new approach in our fight against elder abuse, neglect and exploitation. Today our policies are more reactionary. Tomorrow they must be proactive, coordinated, comprehensive and goal driven. We suggest that a future elder justice policy could be built around the following seven goals addressed at the National Summit:

- Filling Service Gaps;
- Educating the Public;
- Training Professionals;
- Enhancing Adult Protective Services;
- Increasing Prosecution;
- Maximizing Resources; and
- Eliminating Policy Barriers.

NCPEA [National Committee to Prevent Elder Abuse] is proud to be working with Senator Breaux and his staff on his proposed Elder Justice Act. We believe the approach embodied in his proposal is the genuine catalyst that will shift the focus, change the direction and will move us from a federal response to a comprehensive policy on elder justice. We also believe it offers a strong balance in terms of the appropriate role of the federal government. Sometimes government is best when it supports and empowers. Sometimes its role is best when it is the engine developing and driving policy. Both will be needed here if we are to commit to a more serious and focused role of the federal government in elder justice.

> *The reality is the federal response to combating elder abuse and neglect has been piecemeal and ultimately inadequate, as the problem has intensified.*

We must first recognize that elder abuse is a public health, law enforcement and social services crisis. Therefore as a starting point, we must move from the current fragmentation and invisibility that exists within the federal government around elder abuse to one that is focused and will elevate elder justice as a priority.

## Federal Government Must Show Leadership

The federal commitment to the future of elder justice must show leadership through responsibility, accountability, funding and visibility. One approach is offered in Senator Breaux's proposal. He would create Dual Offices of Elder Justice in both the Departments of Health and Human Services and the Department of Justice. This combined with a distinct federal home and a dedicated funding stream for Adult Protective Services is a major step in the right direction.

> *The federal commitment to the future of elder justice must show leadership through responsibility, accountability, funding and visibility.*

We must go beyond what is done inside the federal government in the new approach to elder justice. There must also be an entity created that represents the very valuable state, local, private and multidisciplinary perspectives that are working every day in the field of elder abuse prevention. This public-private entity could be charged with annually assessing the state of elder justice in our nation and could be the sponsoring entity of annual summits on elder justice.

Let me also add that important to any new and expanded federal commitment to elder justice must be regular Congressional oversight of existing and new programs and policies on elder justice to make them as coordinated as possible in the most cost effective manner.

## The Need for Better Reporting

This new commitment to elder justice must absolutely include better data collection and dissemination. The underreporting of elder abuse, neglect and exploitation has several causes. Some are intensely personal relating to the victim. Others are intensely bureaucratic and must be remedied. We can begin by doing research in the areas of data and statistics, determine needs and costs, existing responsibilities and how best to measure outcomes.

As an example, the 15,000 cases of abuse in nursing homes mentioned above came from one source: the annual report of the Long-Term Care Ombudsman Program. It did not necessarily include reports that might have been submitted to state Medicare or Medicaid Fraud age agencies or state licensure or survey offices or even law enforcement. Why? Because there is no identifiable vehicle to collect, analyze or report this other data. This must be remedied. A new federal policy on elder justice must have the authority and the ability to achieve better reporting of abuse cases wherever it may occur.

The case for greater federal resources for elder justice is made much stronger with good data that justifies the need. We strongly believe that we must do more to identify, disseminate and utilize research being done today around elder abuse prevention. Further, where such research does not exist or if new areas of research should emerge, this new elder justice policy must commit dedicated new resources for research. Part of what should be in the research agenda is how to develop and track state-specific training outcomes, research on diverse populations relative to abuse and, something very critical, the development of uniform definitions and standardized reporting criteria. Good research is important for prevention of elder abuse neglect and financial exploitation and therefore is a good investment of federal money.

With respect to future research it is far wiser to sharpen the wheel than to reinvent it. Under a new elder justice policy we should do a basic inventory of what is being done in areas such as intervention, research or community strategies and other multi-disciplinary efforts and activities. These state and local models could be evaluated and recommended for possible national replication.

Extremely pivotal to the research agenda under a new elder justice policy must be a commitment to supporting regular national incidences and prevalence studies. These studies in so many ways could drive the elder justice policy as it could put researchers, front line workers and policymakers on the same page in terms of understanding the statistical extent of the problem as well as possible future trends.

## Justice System Must Play a Primary Role

It is also important that a future elder justice policy support in different ways all the sectors involved in the fight against elder abuse and neglect. This is especially true for law enforcement. To achieve elder justice, the justice system needs to be made more aware of the elder abuse problem. As was noted at the National Summit, elder abuse and neglect must become a priority crime control issue. The justice system including law enforcement, prosecution, correct corrections, judiciary, medical examiners, coroners, public safety officers, victims advocates, APS [Adult Protective Services] workers and Ombudsman must work as a coordinated system to protect victims, hold offenders accountable and prevent future offenses.

In the future, there must also be an emphasis on training on an interdisciplinary, multidisciplinary and cross-educational basis. One of the suggestions from the Summit was a national elder abuse education and training curriculum that could be used by a variety of those involved in the field.

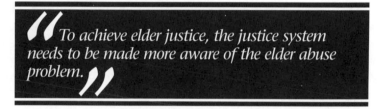

> To achieve elder justice, the justice system needs to be made more aware of the elder abuse problem.

An obvious and critical goal in a future elder justice policy must be the goal of ensuring that elder abusers are never allowed to work in long-term care facilities or board and care facilities. This is a challenging and controversial issue that warrants deeper attention by Congress. Law enforcement must have the ability and tools to achieve swift prosecution against those who might already be employed, but commit abuse against an older person in the facility. In addition, some resources should be committed to training and educating of personnel in these facilities. In the book *Abuse Proofing Your Facility* (Pillemer), it is advanced that there are eight risk factors for someone to become an abuser in a facility; attitudes, burnout, conflict, disruptive/aggressive residents, education and training inadequacy, failure to enforce, gaps in staffing, hiring and screening deficiencies. The key point in this book is that these risk factors are all preventable. Let us commit more time and attention to this.

## Consumers Need to Be Better Informed

We also need to enhance the knowledge base of consumers who are considering long-term care facilities for a loved one. This process to some extent has been started by CMS [the Centers for Medicare and Medicaid Services], but there must be much greater attention paid to distinguishing those facilities with clean records relative to abuse and those who have had problems in the past.

Today elder abuse is any form of mistreatment that results in harm or loss to an older person. It is generally divided into the following categories, yet a sad reality is there seem to be new categories appearing every day:

- Physical abuse;
- Sexual abuse;
- Domestic abuse (involving a family member);
- Psychological;
- Financial; and
- Neglect, including self-neglect.

Elder justice has individual and systemic definitions. From a policy perspective, elder justice consists of efforts to prevent, detect, treat, intervene in and, where appropriate, prosecute elder abuse, neglect and exploitation. From the individual perspective it is the right of older Americans to be free of abuse, neglect and exploitation.

> *To not direct the same level of commitment to elder abuse as to other abuse constitutes a new and deeply troubling form of ageism.*

We believe a new commitment to elder justice is as important as any initiative that has been undertaken to improve the quality of life for seniors in need. It reaffirms our commitment to the priority that federal policy has always given to those most vulnerable as older persons.

## Elder Justice Act Has Far-Ranging Influence

The proposed Elder Justice Act has implications for a variety of programs and initiative, under this Committee's jurisdiction. Social Security is an example. Often it is the misappropriation of the monthly Social Security check by a relative that constitutes abuse. Medicare and Medicaid factor in through the new efforts to address quality of care and abuse prevention in long-term care facilities. This could be a key tool in reducing institutional-based elder abuse. On the other side of the coin is the victim of elder abuse, who may need extended acute care under Medicare to recover from the abuse and the demand that could cause on the program in the future. There is also support for having more Medicaid waiver programs offer community-based services for elder abuse prevention such as respite care. Any new elder justice policy will impact heavily on the Social Services Block Grant, which today is a main source of funding for adult protective services.

A new approach to elder justice could play into some future and pending tax bills including those that would provide incentives to recruit more qualified persons into healthcare, especially those who wish to specialize in geriatric medicine. In addition, as the Committee works further on caregiver legislation, elder justice and the need to provide assistance to caregivers to prevent abuse will come into play. Other areas that were presented at the summit for consideration are the establishment of a national toll-free number dealing with elder justice and a special Elder Justice awareness resolution.

## The Public Must Be Educated About Elder Abuse

A new elder justice policy will rely on public-private partnerships. One area of this will be especially true: we need a sustained national strategic communication program to educate the public especially baby boomers and younger on elder abuse and elder justice. It will involve a national public awareness campaign on elder abuse. It must also work to apply pressure to prevent those occasional advertising campaigns that make light of issues around elder abuse such as exploitation. . . .

This elder justice proposal can also help to address key service gaps that exist today in elder abuse prevention. At the summit, mental health issues were identified as the top need in terms of filling service gaps. The summit called for appropriate and specialized mental health services to be available and accessible. Other service gaps commonly cited include preventive, early intervention and support services.

In closing, 29 years ago as a staffer in the House of Representatives, I worked with former Congressman Mario Biaggi and others including former Senator Walter Mondale on behalf of the first Child Abuse Prevention Act in history. Five years later, as Staff Director of the Subcommittee on Human Services of the House Select Committee on Aging, I organized some of the early hearings held on elder abuse and worked on the later amendments to the Older Americans Act that provided funding for elder abuse prevention. Then, as now, we have a troubling problem of intergenerational abuse in this nation from children to the elderly, which, has only grown worse over time. We must confront all abuse aggressively and with a commitment to reducing it as much as possible.

Our commitment to child abuse and family violence prevention has been good. I believe we have been more remiss with respect to elder abuse prevention. The opportunity to remedy is before us now. It may have been an emerging issue in the late 1970s, but it has fully arrived today. To not direct the same level of commitment to elder abuse as to other abuse constitutes a new and deeply troubling form of ageism.

Let us make elder justice more than a new term. Let's make it a new policy goal as well as a societal aspiration.

# 11

# Dying Seniors
# Need Better Care

## Diane E. Meier and R. Sean Morrison

*Diane E. Meier is a professor of geriatrics, internal medicine, and medical ethics at the Mount Sinai School of Medicine in New York City. She is also director of the Lilian and Benjamin Hertzberg Palliative Care Institute. R. Sean Morrison is director of research at Hertzberg and an associate professor of geriatrics and internal medicine at Mount Sinai.*

Medical professionals and families must accept that death is a natural and inevitable part of growing old. Most people who die in this country are elderly, and they typically die slowly of chronic diseases. While most elderly people are cared for at home by family members as they decline, the vast majority die in hospitals or nursing homes and their quality of life at the end is quite poor. Relieving suffering near the end of life should be just as important as trying to keep someone alive. Society needs to restore the balance of these two goals.

Popular images of death and dying are a jumble of gun violence, young and middle-aged adults on television fighting for life with the help of tubes, intensive care units and modern machinery, and nineteenth century images of feverish mothers or children attended at home by their grieving families and helpless physicians. In reality, these media visions bear little relationship to the actual human experience of dying in the United States. In our society, the overwhelming majority of people who die are elderly. They typically die slowly of chronic

Diane E. Meier and R. Sean Morrison, "Old Age and Care Near the End of Life," *Generations, Journal of the American Society on Aging*, vol. 28, Spring 1999. Copyright © 1999 by American Society on Aging, San Francisco, California, www.asaging.org. Reproduced by permission.

diseases, over long periods of time, with multiple coexisting problems, progressive dependency on others, and heavy care needs met mostly by family members.

## Most Elderly People Die in Facilities

They spend the majority of their final months and years at home but, in most parts of the country, actually die in the hospital or nursing home surrounded by strangers. Many of these deaths become protracted and negotiated processes, with healthcare providers and family members making difficult, often wrenching, decisions about the use or discontinuation of such life-prolonging technologies as feeding tubes, ventilators, and intravenous fluids. There is abundant evidence that the quality of life during the dying process is often poor, characterized by inadequately treated physical distress, fragmented care systems, poor to absent communication between doctors and patients and families, and enormous strains on family caregiver and support systems.

## Dying and Death in the United States

The median age at death in the United States is now 77 years, associated with a steady and linear decline in age-adjusted death rates since 1940. While in 1900 life expectancy at birth was less than 50 years, a girl born today may expect to live to age 79 and a boy to age 73. Those of us reaching 75 years can expect to live another ten (men) to twelve (women) years on average. This dramatic and unprecedented increase in life expectancy (equivalent to that occurring between the Stone Age and the year 1900) is due primarily to decreases in maternal and infant mortality, resulting from improved sanitation and nutrition and effective control of infectious diseases. The result of the changes in demography has been an enormous growth in the number and health of the elderly, so that by the year 2030, 20 percent of the United States' population will be over age 65, as compared to fewer than 5 percent at the turn of the century.

## The Causes of Death Have Changed

While death at the turn of the century was largely attributable to infectious diseases, today the leading causes of death are heart disease, cancer, and stroke. Advances in treatment of atherosclerotic vascular disease and cancer have turned these previously rapidly fatal diseases into chronic illnesses with which people often live for many years before death. In parallel, deaths that occurred at home in the early part of the twentieth century now occur primarily in institutions (57 percent in hospitals and 17 percent in nursing homes). The reasons for its shift in location of death are complex, but they are related to Medicare reimbursement for hospital-based care, with the subsequent rise in the availability of hospitals and hospital beds and in the care burdens of chronicity and functional dependency typically accompanying life-threatening disease in the elderly. The older the patient, the higher the likelihood of death in a nursing home or hospital, with an estimated 58 percent of people over 85 spending at least some time in a nursing home in the last year of life.

> *While death at the turn of the century was largely attributable to infectious diseases, today the leading causes of death are heart disease, cancer, and stroke.*

These statistics, however, hide the fact that the majority of an older person's last months and years is still spent at home in the care of family members, with hospitalization or nursing home placement occurring only near the very end of life. Additionally, national figures such as these hide the substantial regional variation in location of death. In Portland, Oregon, for example, only 35 percent of adult deaths occur in hospitals, as compared to over 80 percent in New York City, a disparity associated at least in part with differences in regional hospital bed supply and availability of adequate community supports for the dying. Finally, national statistics also obscure the variability in the experience of dying that characterizes our highly diverse nation. For example, need for institutionalization or paid formal caregivers in the last months of life is much higher among the poor and women. Similarly, people suffering from cognitive impairment and dementia are much more likely to spend their last days in a nursing home compared to cognitively intact elderly people dying from nondementing illnesses.

## Public Policies Favor Institutionalization

The incentives promoting an institutional—as opposed to home
—death persist despite evidence that patients prefer to die at
home and despite the existence of the Medicare hospice benefit. The hospice benefit was designed to provide substantial professional and material support (medications, equipment) to
families caring for the dying at home for their last six months
of life. Reasons for the low rate of utilization of the Medicare
hospice benefit (serving only 11 percent of adult deaths) vary by
community but include the inhibiting requirements that patients acknowledge that they are dying in order to access the services, that physicians certify a prognosis of six months or less,
and that very few hours (usually four or less) of personal care
home attendants are covered under the benefit. In addition, the
fiscal structure of the Medicare hospice benefit lends itself well
to the predictable trajectory of late-stage cancers or AIDS, but
not so well to the unpredictable chronic course of other common causes of death in the elderly, like congestive heart failure,
chronic lung disease, stroke, and dementing illnesses.

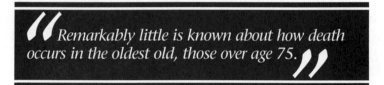

*Remarkably little is known about how death occurs in the oldest old, those over age 75.*

Although death occurs far more commonly in the elderly
than in any other age group, most research on the experience
of dying has examined younger populations. Remarkably little
is known about how death occurs in the oldest old, those over
age 75. The largest and most detailed study of adult hospital
deaths in the United States (the Study to Understand Prognoses
and Preferences for Outcomes and Risks of Treatments, or SUP-
PORT) focused on a relatively young population (the median
age at death in the United States is 77, while the median age in
SUPPORT was only 66 years) and demonstrated a high rate of
untreated pain in the last few days of life, poor doctor-patient
communication about the goals of medical care, and frequent
use of ventilators and intensive care.

There is some evidence that costly "aggressive" and potentially burdensome life-prolonging interventions are less frequently used among the oldest patients, independent of base-
line measures, which may represent a form of implicit rationing

based on age. Other studies have shown consistently high levels of untreated or undertreated pain in the elderly. In one study of elderly cancer patients in nursing homes, 26 percent of patients with daily pain received no analgesic at all, and 16 percent received only Tylenol, a percentage that rose with increasing age and minority status. Another study comparing pain management in cognitively intact versus demented elderly with acute hip fracture also found a high rate of undertreatment of pain in both groups, a phenomenon that worsened with increasing age and cognitive impairment. Similarly [Charles] Cleeland's study of outpatients with cancer found that age and female sex were predictors of undertreatment, a disturbing observation given the dramatic rise in cancer prevalence with increasing age. Finally, chronic pain due to arthritis, other bone and joint disorders, and low back syndrome is probably the most common cause of distress and disability in the elderly, affecting 25–50 percent of community-dwelling older adults and, similar to cancer pain, consistently undertreated. These data suggest that the time before death among elderly people is often characterized by significant physical distress that is neither identified nor properly treated.

## Dependency on Others Is Common for Elderly

Aside from pain and other sources of physical distress, the key characteristic that distinguishes the dying process as experienced by the elderly from that experienced by younger groups, is the nearly universal occurrence of long periods of functional dependency and need for family caregivers in the last months to years of life. SUPPORT, focusing on a younger age cohort, found that 55 percent of patients had persistent and serious family caregiving needs during the course of a terminal illness, a figure that rises exponentially with increasing age. Although the vast majority of caregiving (transportation, homemaker services, personal care, and more skilled nursing care) is done by unpaid family members, paid care supplements or provides the sole source of care for 15 to 20 percent of patients, especially among poor elderly women living alone. Most family caregiving is provided by women (spouses and adult daughters and daughters-in-law), placing significant strains on the physical, emotional, and socioeconomic status of the caregivers. Those ill and dependent patients without family caregivers, or those whose caregivers can no longer provide or afford needed services, are placed in nursing homes, where 20 percent of the over-age-85 population resides.

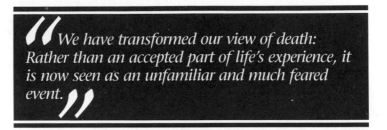

*We have transformed our view of death: Rather than an accepted part of life's experience, it is now seen as an unfamiliar and much feared event.*

Thus, the dying process in the oldest old is characterized by a high prevalence of untreated pain and other symptoms due to chronic conditions and is associated with progressive functional dependency, unpredictable disease course, and extensive family-caregiver needs.

## Mismatch Between Current System and Needs

The current payment system is poorly matched to the needs of the chronically ill and dying elderly. Medicare fee-for-service promotes use of procedure-based payments, hospitalization, and associated specialization and discontinuity of care. Capitated managed care systems [those that receive a fixed amount of money per patient] attempt to avoid seriously ill or dying patients with high-intensity service needs, focusing instead on healthier, lower-cost patient populations. The Medicare hospice benefit was designed for patients with cancer and predictably short life spans who are willing to give up efforts to prolong life and whose families can provide for the majority of their care needs at home. None of these payment systems addresses the long-term-care needs (whether at home or in a nursing home) of chronically ill and functionally dependent individuals whose prognosis is uncertain and whose medical care usually requires simultaneous efforts to prolong life, palliate symptoms, and provide support for functional dependency.

## Medicare Does Not Cover In-Home Help

Medicare does not cover costs of personal care services at home or nursing home costs for the functionally dependent elderly. Instead, these are paid for approximately equally from out-of-pocket and from Medicaid budgetary sources originally intended to provide care for the indigent. Even in nursing homes, standards of care focus on improvement of function and maintenance of weight and nutritional status, and evidence of the decline that accompanies the dying process is typically regarded as a measure of substandard care. Thus, a death in a nursing home is often viewed as evidence, particularly by state regulators, of poor care rather than as an expected outcome for a frail, chronically ill older person. Similarly, quality indicators required in long-term-care settings fail to either assess or reward appropriate attention to such palliative measures as relief of symptoms, spiritual care, and promotion of continuity, with concomitant avoidance of brink-of-death transfers to emergency rooms and hospitals.

## Good News and Bad News

Again, because of unprecedented improvements in material and infant mortality and successes in the control, if not cure, of common chronic diseases, most people who die in the United States are old and frail. They die of chronic, progressive illnesses (such as end-stage heart and lung disease, cancer, stroke, and dementia) with unpredictable clinical courses and prognoses. They have unrecognized and untreated symptoms and an extremely high prevalence of functional dependency and associated family-caregiver burden. Unfortunately, current reimbursement systems are unresponsive to this patient population and their families, failing to provide primary care with continuity, support for family caregivers, and homecare services, and instead promoting fragmented specialized care tied to procedures and hospitals, for lack of any other coherent alternative financing mechanism.

## A Call for Change

This phenomenon has prompted widespread calls for change and reorganization that would ensure accountability for outcomes, processes, and costs of care for the growing population of frail, functionally dependent, and chronically ill elderly in their last phase of life. Since care for a dying person typically includes preventive, life-prolonging, rehabilitation, and palliative measures in varying proportion and intensity based upon the individual patient's needs and preferences, any new model of care will have to be responsive to this range of service requirements.

> *The time has come to restore the balance so that relief of suffering and cure of disease [are] seen as twin obligations of a medical profession that is truly dedicated to patient care.*

For example, an 88-year-old woman with congestive heart failure and deconditioning after hospitalization for pneumonia requires life-prolonging measures (treatment of heart failure, oxygen, and antibiotics), preventive measures (annual influenza vaccination), rehabilitation (home physical therapy to restore independent bed-to-chair mobility), and palliative care (advance care planning, appointment of a healthcare proxy, treatment of depression, diuretics, oxygen, and low-dose opiates for breathing difficulties). Since her daughter works during the day, she also needs a 12-hour-a-day home health aide because she is unable to care for herself independently. Thus, the model of care needed provides simultaneous life-prolonging, palliative, and personal care (for this patient they are nearly one and the same), and, given the difficulty of prognosticating time of death in cases of heart failure, will have to continue to do so for the remainder of the patient's life. . . .

## Care Must Reflect Needs of Patients

Substantial change using approaches such as these will be necessary if the healthcare system is to bear any relationship to the needs of the patients seeking care—patients who are predominantly old and chronically ill and in urgent need of help truly fitted to their needs. Though the problem is daunting, the increase in attention to medical education, research, and clinical service delivery for patients near the end of life is an indication that the need to begin the process of change has been recognized. The next steps, testing new models and seeing what works, will define the new structure of healthcare services for future generations.

Whereas a century ago, virtually everyone died at home, surrounded by family and cared for by physicians whose primary role was the relief of suffering, today the vast majority of Americans die within institutions, surrounded by medical technology and physicians who believe there is nothing else that they can do.

## Society's View of Death Has Been Transformed

While the past one hundred years have seen tremendous advances in the treatment of disease such that previously fatal illnesses like diabetes and congestive heart failure have become chronic conditions, this progress has come at a substantial cost. We have transformed our view of death: Rather than an accepted part of life's experience, it is now seen as an unfamiliar and much feared event. The majority of Americans have never witnessed a loved one die (a common experience at the turn of the century), and physicians are ill-trained and ill-equipped to care for dying patients, and uncomfortable taking responsibility for this care. It is clear that the time has come to restore the balance so that relief of suffering and cure of disease [are] seen as twin obligations of a medical profession that is truly dedicated to patient care.

# 12

# The System of Elderly Care Needs to Accommodate Gay and Lesbian Seniors

## Tamara Thompson

*Tamara Thompson holds a master's of social welfare in gerontology from the University of California–Berkeley. She has published several articles on gay and lesbian aging issues.*

The gay and lesbian baby boomers who came of age during the gay rights movement of the 1960s are the first truly "out" generation. As boomers age, the country will need to care for an unprecedentedly large group of homosexual seniors. Although the need for senior housing, assisted living help, and skilled nursing care will be great, most programs that currently serve the elderly are not sensitive to the needs of lesbian, gay, bisexual, and transgendered (LGBT) people. Changes are needed throughout the elder-care system in order to ensure that gay and lesbian seniors are treated with respect.

For decades, lesbian and gay seniors have been virtually invisible, both within the gay community and society at large. But as the vanguard of the gay rights movement ages and looks to retirement, attention is swiftly turning toward issues affecting the old. Adding to the urgency, the number of LGBT [lesbian, gay, bisexual, and transgendered] seniors—already more than 3 million nationwide—is expected to more than double by

2030 as the baby boom generation ages. Most of them will need senior housing, assisted living help, and skilled nursing care.

"It's time for the community to start paying attention to what it's going to offer for old lesbians and gays," says Nancy Nystrom, a Michigan-based researcher and community organizer who studies and works with old lesbians. "The critical needs that are emerging for old LGBT people are housing that is affordable, medical care that is non-discriminatory and safe, and social support structures that include the old within all facets of LGBT life."

## Queer Seniors Face Ageism in Gay Community

Queer elders also face the additional challenge of confronting agephobia within a very youth-oriented gay community. "Older lesbians and gays experience a double whammy—they're marginalized in the LGBT community for being old, and in the senior community for being gay," says Terry Kaelber, executive director of Senior Action in a Gay Environment (SAGE), the nation's oldest and largest social services organization for lesbian and gay seniors.

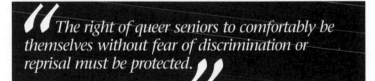

*The right of queer seniors to comfortably be themselves without fear of discrimination or reprisal must be protected.*

SAGE has chapters throughout the United States and Canada and sponsors an annual National Conference on Aging in the LGBT Communities to highlight LGBT aging issues. Lesbian and gay aging is finally showing up on the radar of mainstream organizations, too. The American Society on Aging has created a Lesbian and Gay Aging Issues Network and now offers an extensive track of workshops devoted to LGBT issues during its annual conference each year. Workshops range from elder sexuality, to late-life legal planning, to long-term care for LGBT people, to mental health issues associated with aging.

All signs say that the need is great.

A recent study done by SAGE in conjunction with the Brookdale Center on Aging at Hunter College in Manhattan found that gay and lesbian seniors are "twice as likely [66 percent vs. 33 percent] as the general population of seniors to live alone." The reason is no big mystery: More than 75 percent of LGBT people never have children, and others are estranged from their extended families because of their lifestyles. But living alone doesn't just mean isolation and loneliness—it can mean far worse.

## Isolation Leads to Higher Dementia Risk

In 2001, scientists at the Stockholm Gerontology Research Center at Karolinska Institute in Sweden found that the more socially isolated seniors are, the more likely they are to develop dementia. The study—comprised of 1,200 men and women who were over age 75—showed that those who live alone, have no friends or have bad relationships with their children are up to 60 percent more likely to develop dementia than those who have more socially satisfying encounters.

That statistic has staggering implications, but it's also just the tip of the iceberg. Living alone is just one of the challenges that aging gays and lesbians face because of who they are. For example:

- Queer seniors who enter mainstream care facilities often face discrimination and abuse if they remain open about their sexual identities. Few caregivers have been trained to recognize and be sensitive to the needs of gay and lesbian elders, and homophobic peers can quickly create a hostile environment for an LGBT person who is out.
- Traditional facilities that serve the elderly don't generally make provisions for gay and lesbian seniors. Physical contact between same-sex individuals is routinely discouraged in care-home settings, and couples are often separated. By contrast, many mainstream facilities allow straight, married couples to share private rooms.
- LGBT people face additional emotional challenges in coping with death of a partner because caregivers and families may not recognize or acknowledge the significance of their loss—or their right to inherit shared property.
- In many states, hospitalized gays and lesbians are still routinely denied visits from their longtime partners, adding even more stress to a health crisis.

There are many horror stories, but there is progress, too. SAGE in particular has made great strides in outreach to LGBT seniors and their caregivers. Besides sensitivity training for health care professionals, SAGE offers friendly visitor programs for homebound seniors, social clubs, a drop-in center, social worker visits and scores of other activities and initiatives. SAGE is an advocate for queer seniors everywhere, but most of its work is centered in New York City.

Although awareness is slowly growing nationwide, queer seniors in most parts of the country remain mostly overlooked and underserved. It's high time that changed. Social workers, medical professionals, nursing home employees, at-home aides and others who work with seniors should receive training so that they can understand LGBT seniors and their needs. The formal policies of nursing homes, board and care facilities and hospitals should be updated to embrace sexual diversity so that they no longer discriminate—whether intentionally or not—on the basis of orientation. Above all, the right of queer seniors to comfortably be themselves without fear of discrimination or reprisal must be protected.

# Glossary

**activities of daily living (ADLs):** Activities necessary for individuals to take care of themselves independently. ADLs include bathing, eating, dressing, grooming, going to the toilet, taking medication, and transferring from a bed to chair.

**aging in place:** Growing old in one's own home rather than in a nursing home or other facility for the elderly.

**assisted-living facility:** Housing for older people who cannot live on their own but do not need as much care as a nursing home provides. People who live in assisted-living facilities usually have their own private apartments and receive help with such things as medication management, bathing, and housekeeping. Assisted-living facilities are typically very expensive, and government programs such as Medicaid and Medicare do not help pay for them.

**baby boomers:** The 76 million Americans born between 1946 and 1964, following World War II. "Boomers" are the country's largest demographic group, and their aging will have profound consequences for the country in terms of social services, housing, and health care expenditures. The last of the baby boomers will reach age fifty-five in 2019, and it is estimated that 20 percent of the U.S. population will be over sixty-five by 2030.

**elder abuse:** Any physical, psychological, financial, or sexual mistreatment of an older adult. Also includes neglect, which is the withholding of care or necessities from an individual, and self-neglect, the inability of an elderly person to take care of themself.

**hospice:** A philosophy of caring for terminally ill people that is characterized by concern for relieving symptoms and pain, increasing general well-being, and providing spiritual comfort for those who are dying.

**institutionalization:** A term used to describe the long-term placement of individuals in medical settings or mental facilities. When the term is applied to the elderly, it typically refers to their being cared for in nursing homes or hospitals.

**instrumental activities of daily living (IADLs):** Activities that are not necessary for basic self-care, but which are still very important to everyday life. IADLs include the ability to use a telephone, prepare meals, shop for food and clothing, do housework, use transportation, and handle financial matters.

**long-term care (LTC):** A wide range of supports and services provided to individuals who are unable to live independently because of chronic illness or disability. Although LTC may be provided in a person's home, most LTC facilities are nursing homes.

**Medicaid:** A government health insurance program for low-income people. It is funded jointly by federal and state money and is administered by the states, each of which has its own Medicaid program. In California, Medicaid is known as MediCal. To qualify for Medicaid, individuals must pass a means test to prove that they are poor. The biggest expense of Medicaid is nursing home care for elderly people. In 2002 Medicaid paid for 47 percent of the total long-term care costs nationwide.

**Medicare:** The federal government's health insurance program for the elderly and disabled. Established in 1965 as a set of amendments to Social Security, Medicare is available to anyone sixty-five or older, younger people with disabilities, and people with permanent kidney failure. The program has two parts: Part A (hospital insurance) and Part B (Medicare insurance, which helps cover doctors' services, outpatient care, and some other services that Part A does not cover). A recently added prescription drug benefit will take effect in 2006. Medicare does not pay for nursing home stays longer than thirty days, a major issue of financial concern for the elderly. In 2003 Medicare provided health coverage for 40 million Americans. Enrollment is expected to reach 77 million by 2031, when the baby boom generation is fully enrolled. Medicare is administered by the Centers for Medicare and Medicaid Services (CMS) in the U.S. Department of Health and Human Services.

**medigap insurance:** Private insurance policies that cover the difference between what Medicare pays for and what is actually charged for medical services.

**nursing home:** Any residential facility that provides some degree of medical care to residents. There are three levels of care: skilled, intermediate, and extended. A skilled nursing facility offers a full range of medical treatment and personal care to residents. An intermediate care facility offers health-related care for patients who need a lower level of assistance. An extended care facility is primarily a transitional or rehabilitation facility that offers short-term convalescence after a hospital stay.

**Older Americans Act (OAA):** A 1965 federal law that authorized and established funding for a wide variety of direct services for older adults, such as senior centers, nutrition programs, case management, and information and referral programs.

***Olmstead* decision:** A landmark 1999 Supreme Court ruling that interpreted the Americans with Disabilities Act (ADA) to mean that elderly and disabled individuals should be allowed to live in the least restrictive setting possible. The *Olmstead* decision has caused a shift away from the institutionalization of the elderly and toward more home-based care.

**palliative care:** Any type of medical care that focuses on reducing the severity of pain and slowing the progress of disease rather than trying to cure it. The goal of palliative care—sometimes called "comfort care"—is to improve the quality of life rather than prolong it.

**pay-go system:** Short for "pay-as-you-go," an approach to paying for Social Security in which today's workers contribute money that is used to pay for benefits for individuals who are currently retired. Under the pay-go system, current workers pay for current benefits, rather than the money being set aside to pay for their own future benefits.

**skilled nursing facility (SNF):** A residential care facility for people who require constant medical attention but at a lower level of care than in a hospital. Usually the residents are elderly, but younger people who need skilled medical care often reside there as well. About 80 percent of skilled nursing facilities in the United States are run by for-profit companies.

**Social Security:** The federal government program that pays retirement benefits to the elderly and death benefits to surviving family members. Social Security was created in 1935 as part of President Franklin Delano Roosevelt's New Deal. The program is funded by a payroll tax that is half paid by employers and half by workers. Retirement benefits are paid monthly according to a formula based on how much a person earned over their lifetime. Social Security operates under a pay-go system; current year benefits are paid from current taxes. Because of the large number of baby boomers that will soon retire, taxes are not expected to cover expenses by 2015. There is a great deal of debate about what should be done. One of the most likely scenarios is the partial privatization of Social Security through the creation of individual accounts. Current proposals call for individuals to be allowed to use these accounts to put some of their Social Security money into the stock market. There is much controversy surrounding this plan. Other ideas include reducing benefit payments or again raising the age at which people can collect Social Security.

**supplemental security income (SSI):** A federal program administered by Social Security that provides a monthly payment to low-income disabled individuals who cannot work and who have no other income. To qualify for SSI, individuals must pass a means test to prove that they are poor. Many elderly people receive SSI, which is meant to help pay for basic necessities such as food, shelter, and clothing. In most states, being eligible for SSI means an individual is also entitled to medical coverage through Medicaid.

# Organizations to Contact

The editors have compiled the following list of organizations concerned with the issues presented in this book. The descriptions are derived from materials provided by the organizations. All have publications or information available for interested readers. The list was compiled on the date of publication of the present volume; the information provided here may change. Be aware that many organizations take several weeks or longer to respond to inquiries, so allow as much time as possible.

**AARP**
601 E St. NW, Washington, DC 20049
(800) 424-3410
e-mail: member@aarp.org • Web site: www.aarp.org

AARP, formerly known as the American Association of Retired Persons, is a nonpartisan association that seeks to improve the aging experience for all Americans. It is committed to the preservation of Social Security and Medicare. AARP publishes the magazine *Modern Maturity* and the newsletter *AARP Bulletin.* Issue statements and congressional testimony can be found at the Web site.

**Administration on Aging (AOA)**
330 Independence Ave. SW, Washington, DC 20201
(202) 619-0724 • fax: (202) 357-3555
e-mail: aoainfo@aoa.gov • Web site: www.aoa.dhhs.gov

The AOA works with a number of organizations, senior centers, and local service providers to help older people remain independent. It also works to protect the rights of the elderly, prevent crime and violence against older persons, and investigate health care fraud. AOA's publications include fact sheets on issues such as age discrimination, elder abuse, and Alzheimer's disease. Additional publications are available through AOA's National Aging Information Center.

**Alzheimer's Association**
919 North Michigan Ave., Suite 1100, Chicago, IL 60611-1676
(800) 272-3900 • fax: (312) 335-1110
e-mail: info@alz.org • Web site: www.alz.org

The Alzheimer's Association is committed to finding a cure for Alzheimer's and helping those affected by the disease. The association funds research into the causes and treatments of Alzheimer's disease and provides education and support for people diagnosed with the condition, their families, and caregivers. Position statements and fact sheets are available at its Web site.

### American Geriatrics Society (AGS)
350 Fifth Ave., Suite 801, New York, NY 10118
(212) 308-1414 • fax: (212) 832-8646
e-mail: info@americangeriatrics.org
Web site: www.americangeriatrics.org

The AGS is a professional organization of health care providers that aims to improve the health and well-being of all older adults. AGS helps shape attitudes, policies, and practices regarding health care for older people. The society's publications include the book *The American Geriatrics Society's Complete Guide to Aging and Health*, the magazines *Journal of the American Geriatrics Society* and *Annals of Long-Term Care: Clinical Care and Aging*, and *The AGS Newsletter*.

### American Society on Aging
833 Market St., Suite 511, San Francisco, CA 94103-1824
(415) 974-9600 • fax: (415) 974-0300
e-mail: info@asaging.org • Web site: www.asaging.org

The American Society on Aging is an organization of health care and social service professionals, researchers, educators, businesspersons, senior citizens, and policy makers that is concerned with all aspects of aging and works to enhance the well-being of older individuals. Its publications include the bimonthly newspaper *Aging Today* and the quarterly journal *Generations*.

### Family Caregiver Alliance (FCA)
80 Montgomery St., Suite 1100, San Francisco, CA 94104
(800) 445-8106 • fax: (415) 434-3508
e-mail: info@caregiver.org • Web site: www.caregiver.org

Founded in 1977, FCA is a community-based nonprofit organization that serves the needs of families and friends providing long-term care at home. FCA offers programs at the national, state, and local levels to support and assist caregivers and is a public voice for caregivers through education, services, research, and advocacy. Its Web site offers a wide range of information on caregiver issues and resources, including numerous fact sheets, policy papers, and other publications.

### Medicare Rights Center (MRC)
1460 Broadway, 17th Fl., New York, NY 10036
(212) 869-3850 • fax: (212) 869-3532
e-mail: info@medicarerights.org • Web site: www.medicarerights.org

The MRC is a national organization that helps ensure that older adults receive affordable quality health care. It publishes a wide variety of Medicare materials, including a series of self-help pamphlets on Medicare issues and numerous booklets on Medicare-related topics.

### National Association for Home Care (NAHC)
228 Seventh St. SE, Washington, DC 20003
(202) 547-7424 • fax: (202) 547-3540
e-mail: pr@nahc.org • Web site: www.nahc.org

The NAHC believes that Americans should receive health care and social services in their own homes. It represents home care agencies, hospices, and home care aide organizations. NAHC publishes the quarterly newspaper *Homecare News* and the monthly magazine *Caring*.

**National Association of Area Agencies on Aging (N4A)**
1730 Rhode Island Ave. NW, Suite 1200, Washington, DC 20036
(202) 872-0888 • fax: (202) 872-0057
Web site: www.n4a.org

The N4A on Aging is the umbrella organization for the 655 area agencies on aging in the United States. Its mission is to help older people and those with disabilities live with dignity and choices in their homes and communities for as long as possible. The N4A Web site provides links to Area Agencies on Aging in all states as well as to other government organizations that serve seniors. It also acts as a portal for the Eldercare Locator, a national toll-free number to assist older people and their families in finding community services for seniors anywhere in the country.

**National Center on Elder Abuse (NCEA)**
1201 Fifteenth St. NW, Suite 350, Washington, DC 20005
(202) 898-2586 • fax: (202) 898-2583
e-mail: ncea@nasua.org • Web site: www.elderabusecenter.org

The NCEA is a gateway to resources on elder abuse, neglect, and exploitation. The NCEA is funded by the U.S. Administration on Aging. The center offers news and resources; collaborates on research; provides consultation, education, and training; identifies and provides information about promising practices and interventions; answers inquiries and requests for information; operates a Listserv forum for professionals; and advises on program and policy development.

**National Citizens' Coalition for Nursing Home Reform**
1424 Sixteenth St. NW, Suite 202, Washington, DC 20036-2211
(202) 332-2275 • fax: (202) 332-2949
e-mail: nccnhr@nccnhr.org • Web site: www.nccnhr.org

The National Citizens' Coalition for Nursing Home Reform provides information and leadership on federal and state regulatory and legislative policy development and strategies to improve nursing home care and life for residents. Publications include the book *Nursing Homes: Getting Good Care There*, NCCNHR's newsletter *Quality Care Advocate*, and fact sheets on issues such as abuse and neglect, restraints use, and how to choose a nursing home.

**National Committee to Preserve Social Security and Medicare**
10 G St. NE, Suite 600, Washington, DC 20004
(800) 966-1935 • fax: (202) 216-0451
e-mail: general@ncpssm.org • Web site: www.ncpssm.org

The National Committee to Preserve Social Security and Medicare is a nonprofit, nonpartisan membership organization. Through advocacy, education, services, and grassroots efforts, the committee works to ensure a secure retirement for all Americans. Its Web site is a good place to find information and analyses regarding Social Security, Medicare, and other retirement issues.

**National Council on the Aging (NCOA)**
300 D St. SW, Suite 801, Washington, DC 20024
(202) 479-1200 • fax: (202) 479-0735
e-mail: info@ncoa.org • Web site: www.ncoa.org

The NCOA is an association of organizations and professionals dedicated to promoting the dignity, self-determination, well-being, and contributions of older people. It advocates business practices, societal attitudes, and public policies that promote vital aging. NCOA's quarterly magazine, *Journal of the National Council on the Aging*, provides tools and insights for community service organizations.

**National Hospice and Palliative Care Organization (NHPCO)**
1700 Diagonal Rd., Suite 625, Alexandria, VA 22314
(703) 837-1500 • fax: (703) 837-1233
e-mail: nhpco_info@nhpco.org • Web site: www.nhpco.org

The NHPCO (originally the National Hospice Organization) was founded in 1978 to educate the public about the benefits of hospice care for the terminally ill and their families. It seeks to promote the idea that with the proper care and pain medication, the terminally ill can live out their lives comfortably and in the company of their families. The organization opposes euthanasia and assisted suicide. It conducts educational and training programs for administrators and caregivers in numerous aspects of hospice care. The NHPCO publishes grief and bereavement guides, brochures such as *Hospice Care: A Consumer's Guide to Selecting a Hospice Program* and *Communicating Your End-of-Life Wishes*, and the book *Hospice Care: A Celebration*.

**Senior Action in a Gay Environment (SAGE)**
305 Seventh Ave., 16th Fl., New York, NY 10001
(212) 741-2247 • fax: (212) 366-1947
e-mail: sageusa@aol.com • Web site: www.sageusa.org

SAGE is the world's largest and oldest organization devoted specifically to meeting the needs of aging LGBT (lesbian, gay, bisexual, and transgendered) people. SAGE provides direct services to LGBT seniors in New York City and works to increase awareness of gay aging through education and advocacy throughout the United States.

# Bibliography

## Books

| | |
|---|---|
| Henry Aaron, John Shoven, and Benjamin Friedman, eds. | *Should the United States Privatize Social Security?* Boston: MIT Press, 1999. |
| Stuart Altman and David Shactman | *Policies for an Aging Society.* Baltimore: Johns Hopkins University Press, 2002. |
| Sue Blevins | *Medicare's Midlife Crisis.* Washington, DC: Cato Institute, 2001. |
| Ira Byock | *Dying Well: Peace and Possibilities at the End of Life.* New York: Riverhead, 1998. |
| Ken Dychtwald | *Age Power: How the Twenty-First Century Will Be Ruled by the New Old.* New York: Penguin Putnam, 1999. |
| Lita Epstein | *The Complete Idiot's Guide to Social Security.* Indianapolis: Alpha, 2002. |
| Peter Ferrara and Michael Tanner | *Common Cents, Common Dreams—a Layman's Guide to Social Security Privatization.* Washington, DC: Cato Institute, 1998. |
| Donald Gelfand | *The Aging Network: Programs and Services.* 5th ed. New York: Springer, 1999. |
| Neil Gilbert | *Transformation of the Welfare State: The Silent Surrender of Public Responsibility.* New York: Oxford University Press, 2002. |
| Margaret Morganroth Gullette | *Aged by Culture.* Chicago: University of Chicago Press, 2004. |
| Mary Hird | *Elder Abuse, Neglect, and Maltreatment: What Can Be Done to Stop It.* Pittsburgh: Dorrance, 2003. |
| Harry Moody | *Aging: Concepts and Controversies.* 3rd ed. Thousand Oaks, CA: Pine Forge, 2000. |
| Patricia Smith et al. | *Alzheimer's for Dummies.* Hoboken, NJ: Wiley, 2003. |
| U.S. Department of Transportation | *Transportation for a Maturing Society.* Washington, DC: U.S. Department of Transportation, 1997. |

## Periodicals

| | |
|---|---|
| Edmund Andrews | "Economic View: Social Security Reform, with One Big Catch," *New York Times*, December 12, 2004. |

106

Associated Press | "Democrats Say Medicare Law Could Eat into Social Security Benefits," *Boston Herald*, July 21, 2004.

Robert M. Ball | "How to Fix Social Security? It Doesn't Have to Be Hard," *Aging Today*, March/April 2004.

Wendy Bonafazi | "Who Pays for Long Term Care?" *Contemporary Long Term Care*, October 1998.

James J. Callahan Jr. | "Giving the Elderly Options on Independent Living," *Boston Globe*, November 24, 2002.

*Consumer Reports* | "How Will You Pay for Your Old Age?" October 1997.

Stephen Crystal | "Elder Abuse: The Latest Crisis," *Public Interest*, 1987.

Robert B. Friedland | "Caregivers and Long-Term Care Needs in the 21st Century: Will Public Policy Meet the Challenge?" Issue brief, Long-Term Care Financing Project, Georgetown University, Washington, DC, 2004.

Victor Fuchs | "Health Care for the Elderly: How Much? Who Will Pay for It?" *Health Affairs*, January/February 1999.

William Gale | "Retirement Saving and Long-Term Care Needs: An Overview," Retirement Security Project, Brookings Institution and Tax Policy Center, 2004.

Vicki Haddock | "Seniors Can't Go Home Again—Medi-Cal Rules Force State's Elderly into Costly Nursing Facilities," *San Francisco Chronicle*, August 1, 2004.

Health Policy Institute | "Medicaid and an Aging Population," Fact sheet, Long-Term Care Financing Project, Georgetown University, Washington, DC, 2004.

Marsha King | "Concerns of Elder Gays—Aging Poses New Healthcare, Legal Challenges for Partners," *Seattle Times*, October 7, 2001.

N.R. Kleinfield | "Lillian and Julia—a Twilight of Fear: Bowed by Age and Battered by an Addicted Nephew," *New York Times*, December 12, 2004.

Paul Krugman | "Inventing a Crisis," *New York Times*, December 7, 2004.

Michael Lemonick and Alice Park-Mankato | "The Nun Study—How One Scientist and 678 Sisters Are Helping Unlock the Secrets of Alzheimer's," *Time*, May 14, 2001.

Phillip Longman | "Fixing Social Security," *Fortune*, November 1, 2004.

*New York Times* | "How Not to Save Social Security," September 23, 2004.

Julie Phillips — "Baby Boomers Come of Age and Generation X Sounds Off," *Utne Reader*, March/April 1994.

Barbara Stucki and Janemarie Mulvey — "Can Aging Boomers Avoid Nursing Homes?" *Consumers' Research Magazine*, August 2000.

Shankar Vedantam — "Reagans' Experience Alters Outlook for Alzheimer's Patients," *Washington Post*, June 14, 2004.

# Index